HOPE
IN THE
Hard

Hope in the Hard

Action Steps for Navigating Hardships

Christina Smallwood

©2025 All Rights Reserved. No portion of this book may be reproduced, stored in a retrieval system, or transmitted in any form or by any means—electronic, mechanical, photocopy, recording, scanning, or other—except for brief quotations in critical reviews or articles without the prior permission of the author.

Published by Game Changer Publishing

Paperback ISBN: 978-1-967424-85-6

Hardcover ISBN: 978-1-967424-86-3

Digital ISBN: 978-1-967424-87-0

www.GameChangerPublishing.com

This book is dedicated to my husband, who has stood so incredibly by my side as we navigated the most unimaginable hardships together. I am forever grateful for your hand to hold, your shoulder to cry on, the unwavering tough love when I needed it (not when I wanted it), and the endless support and encouragement you give me every single day. Thank you for allowing me a safe space to feel all the emotions and go at my own pace through them.

Words will never do justice to describe how much I love you and how grateful I am for you leading our home the way you do.

All my love & gratitude,
Munks

Read This First

Huge thanks for buying and reading my book.
Let's stay connected!
I have a few great business resources & freebies for you!

HOPE
IN THE
Hard

CHRISTINA SMALLWOOD

Foreword

"HOPE IN THE HARD"

It was a crisp early morning on October 31st, 1984. My husband and I were sound asleep. I was big and pregnant, and my due date was a couple of days away. Suddenly, we were both awakened by a loud pop, like a water balloon had exploded. I sat straight up and excitedly said, "Frank, I think my water just broke!" Frank jumped up and shouted, "Let's go!" as he ran into our three-year-old son's room to get him. We packed up the car, our son Frankie wrapped in a blanket, and off we headed to the hospital.

We were a baseball family who had just returned from the ball season in Cincinnati to our off-season home in California. We were excited to welcome baby Pastore No.2 to our family. We didn't want to know the sex of the baby beforehand; we were old-fashioned in that sense. We had a few different names picked out, but nothing concrete.

I had labored for several hours with my son, but this baby was coming out quick! My doctor barely came into the delivery room, and the nurses were telling me to go ahead and push! In three pushes, our baby girl made her grand entrance. They put her on my chest, and she immediately cried, looking for my breast, like she was starving. Christina Ann Pastore was hungry, expressive, and tenacious. I remember thinking, *This one is going to be a firecracker.*

My beautiful daughter is indeed setting the world on fire. As you will read, she has been through many of life's ups and downs, from being a rebellious minister's kid to all of the losses she has endured. It hasn't been an easy road, and as her mother, there were times I wanted to cover my eyes. Our relationship has evolved over the years. At one time, she cut me out of her life for a year. While it was a terribly painful time, it was also a time of so much growth for her, and me as well. She was determined to do the work necessary for her emotional growth and development.

During that time, I witnessed her morphing from "the rebellious child" into the most wonderful, strong woman. Watching her do that has opened my eyes to a greater quality of life. It's so sad that there are so many people who will never grow their souls or experience freedom from their past failures, traumas, and demons.

I love how Christina Smallwood is a force for good. I love that she is willing to be vulnerable. I love how she cares about helping others through life's challenges. I love how she loves her husband and children. I love how she loves God.

Life is hard, and so often, we fall short. My prayer is that you will be encouraged as you read through my daughter's journey. Her dad and I never lost faith in her. We always saw her willingness and determination to do the right thing, and sometimes, it was a winding road!

Lastly, my prayer is that you **never** lose **hope**. Someone recently asked me, "What is hope?"

I replied, "Hope is knowing God has you in His hands, that He loves you, and has a plan for your life." We have hope because we have a Creator who never gives up on us, even at our weakest moments.

– Gina Pastore,
Christina's mom

Contents

Read This First	1
Foreword	5
Introduction	11
Chapter 1 *How a Self-Saboteur Was Born*	17
Chapter 2 *Grief*	39
Chapter 3 *Humor as a Hiding Place*	53
Chapter 4 *Inadequacy*	67
Chapter 5 *People Pleasing*	81
Chapter 6 *Numbing*	91
Chapter 7 *Guilt & Shame*	107
Chapter 8 *Black Sheep, but Make It Pink*	117
Conclusion	127

Introduction

You may look at the cover of this book and see me all dolled up in a sparkly dress, seemingly without a care in the world, like everything has just gone the way I wanted it to. From the outside, you see I'm happily married with three beautiful children, and you see us living our dream life in Southern California. You may assume that overnight, I grew a social media following and became a celebrity hairstylist and that it was a cakewalk to become one of the top income earners, leading one of the largest teams in the industry. But as the saying goes, "Everyone is fighting a battle you know nothing about." Let me take you back to a moment when everything felt like it was utterly hopeless...

  I had recently come off the high of celebrating my first wedding anniversary and my twenty-eigth birthday. My husband and I were secretly trying to conceive (to hopefully surprise our family with the news around the holidays), my career as a hairstylist was flourishing, and we were saving up for our first home.

Life was finally calm and seemed to be on track for a smooth future when, the week of Thanksgiving, I received an unforgettable knock at the door that delivered life-changing news: My dad had been in a horrible accident and had been airlifted to a nearby hospital, where he died after spending four weeks in a coma.

Hopelessness kicked in, but it didn't reach its ultimate low until about six months later. During that time, we received news that I was infertile, and we began the adoption process, officially becoming "adoptive hopefuls." Then, after receiving a match, we got the news that our baby girl had been born nine weeks early via emergency C-section, and she had suffered brain injuries. The all-time low of hopelessness hit when the doctors told me, "She might not ever walk or talk."

It was by far the hardest year of my life. It felt like someone had tossed us into the heavy cycle and hit start. As soon as we felt like we might be able to come up for air, another wave of grief and hard news came crashing down on us.

If you're reading this, I'm guessing you've been in a "hard" too. Maybe your story is not the same, but you've felt the same pain—different circumstances, but the same sense of overwhelm. Trust me, I get it. It's like a club you never wanted to be a part of, and I'm here to tell you that you are not alone.

There is hope in the hard, my friend.

Whenever you read the word "hope" in these pages, I want you to know that it is not just a concept or a feeling. The action steps of hope, for me, have led to a relationship with Jesus Christ. He is my salvation, my strength in every season (even when I didn't realize), and the one who has carried me through the hardest valleys. In Him, I've been able to lay down the baggage I once held so tightly, and in return, I've been made new. It would be impossible to tell my story without first telling you about Him. Pursuing a relationship with Jesus is not only the foundation of my own healing, but the invitation I extend to you as you walk through your own hard places.

Over the years, I've encountered all the emotions that accompany facing hardships: grief, anger, people-pleasing, resentment, numbness, and feeling like a black sheep, and I've emerged with realizations I wish I had known back then. In this book, I'm sharing everything I've learned about navigating the darkest times and coming out stronger on the other side. This book isn't for me to divulge my despair diaries; it's to serve as a guide for others with real, actionable steps—like a blueprint for how to get through it.

Here's what you can expect. Each chapter highlights a different emotion that accompanies hardship because not everyone who faces each struggle will be met with the same emotions. I decided to tackle it this way so that if you meet someone who is struggling with grief, they can simply start with the chapter about grief. Anyone can pick it up at any time and read the chapter that most resonates with what they are going through.

What I want people to walk away thinking about is not only that you're going to get through it, but also that it will hopefully help you **connect the dots** on past traumas from your childhood. As I coach women every single day, I realize that the majority of the issues we face aren't necessarily new; they are just repackaged in adult form. We are on cycles and stuck in emotional patterns. I remember the emotions of life feeling very gray, confusing, and overwhelming. They felt like I would always be trapped in them, if that makes sense. Then, once I went to therapy and connected the dots, everything turned to color and started to make sense.

Learning about yourself is something most people don't take the time to do. It took me until I was thirty-five and truly just **over my own crap.**

I divulge and dig deep into all the different **hard** things I've been through, including things I've never spoken about publicly or shared on my social media (where I am an extremely open book). My goal is to provide you with the same guidance that I needed, and in a way that's approachable, compassionate, and straight from the heart of someone who has faced something similar and lived to tell the tale.

The road won't be easy, but I promise you that the most beautiful perspective comes from getting to the other side of your obstacles. As I continue to connect with women who are struggling every single day, I am reminded, on a regular basis, that it's less about surviving one day at a time and more about taking it one step at a time. I like to use the word "step" because it requires an understanding that **hope** is an action.

I want you to pause for a moment, take a deep breath, close your eyes, and think about you. What is currently causing you pain? What are you struggling with? Find a corresponding chapter and start there. If sitting with your thoughts and feelings is difficult, I urge you to check out the chapter on Numbing or Avoiding. I give you permission to go completely out of order, which allows me to meet you where you're at and not the other way around.

This book will mean absolutely nothing if it doesn't inspire you to connect the dots and take action. The first step in hope is identifying exactly what it is that you're going through. Whatever demon you're facing, once you identify it and realize it's not going to last forever, it loses its power, and you've begun your first step of hope.

CHAPTER One

HOW A SELF-SABOTEUR WAS BORN

I was in the principal's office yet again, being questioned about what had happened with the softball that had gone through the window of the girls' locker room. I remember the teacher telling me, "You are changing. What is happening to you?"

At this moment in my life, I felt sheltered, but I was also outgrowing the bubble that my parents had me in. It just seemed like I was constantly in trouble, constantly being questioned. All of the conversations with my parents were about what I was doing wrong, how I could have done better, and why I wasn't applying myself.

I felt like I wasn't going to be able to escape things being hard, so I started looking for acceptance. I was looking for a way to be someone who would be treated the same way that my brother was. I grew up in a home where I was the youngest. I was deemed a quintessential rebellious pastor's kid. I didn't want to meet up to these expectations, but several titles and labels were constantly put on me: "strong-willed," "accident-prone," and "forgetful." While the majority of people will have labels put on them, I share so you have an understanding of who I am and how I grew up. Words matter, and whether it seems harmless or not, the labels we give ourselves can have a long-lasting stronghold over us, even subconsciously.

I was definitely a bit obnoxious and loud, but socially, I was a butterfly. I loved meeting new people, experiencing new situations, and making new friends. Perhaps I looked at every new person as exciting because they hadn't been around long enough to learn the labels I'd been given. I got a fresh start with each new person. I was way too young to realize at the time what the draw to **new** environments was, but now I get a sense of why I was constantly shifting after-school activities and quitting the moment something got hard to start something new. Being "new" was easier than facing the "hard" realization that these labels just seemed to follow me everywhere I went. I didn't realize until I was in my thirties that if I wanted the labels to change, I had to change my habits. Seems like common sense, but when you're stuck in a cycle, you don't realize you have a choice to end it.

At the time, I didn't realize the effect that these labels would have on me.

I remember doing things and realizing the different ways that I could get attention inside and outside of my house. If I could get away with something and people would like me for it, then I was going to do it.

Growing up, I was constantly compared to my brother. Here's a little backstory on him. He was three and a half years older and four grades ahead, and we were very, very, very close when we were younger. But as soon as junior high hit, I became interested in boys, started making bad decisions, and began watching TV shows that he didn't like. I was convinced that *Saved by the Bell* was exactly how high school was. Since he was already in high school, he constantly got upset with me, saying, "No, that's not how it is."

I realized early on that he wasn't going to be one of my best friends, but I loved our relationship at home. One of the things that really stood out to me was that my brother always got really good grades. I got really good grades, too, until I was introduced to boys. Then, I kind of stopped caring and stopped applying myself in school because that wasn't fulfilling me in a way that I felt like I needed to be fulfilled.

The first time I brought home a B- on my report card, my parents sat me down, asked me why I'd done so poorly, and then lectured me. And this would be me applying myself at around fifty to sixty percent in school. I definitely found that I was more inclined to be social at school and really more into that aspect of it. I also developed major crushes. I became obsessive. I like to say I was always on a quest.

My first quest was to get a boyfriend. My brother was not interested in things like that at all, which made me look very different from him in my parents' eyes. He was also never in trouble. We're just opposites. In my sophomore year of high school, I went to a private school; I always went to private schools. That's how I grew up. I changed schools multiple times growing up, and I was sort of always the new girl.

When I was in kindergarten, we moved, and I went to a new school. Then I went to a *different* school for first grade. Then we moved to Ohio, and I got held back. I guess I was too young for the class because I have an "October birthday." I remember the school saying, "She still wants to nap, so we're going to hold her back." Not only was I in a new state—a California girl in Ohio—but I was also sent back to kindergarten. That was pretty devastating to me, but I ended up getting my first little boyfriend, Seth. He gave me a big yellow ring from a vending machine, and that seemed to make me completely fine with going *back* to kindergarten. I let him cheat off of me because I had already done the curriculum, and I became like his little mentor.

Even at a young age, I realized the tone being set for me—*I didn't quite fit in where they placed me.* When we moved back to California, I attended a different elementary school and stayed there through junior high. After graduating from middle school, I went to a completely different high school, a few cities away. It may as well have been in a different state—I didn't know anybody.

Part of that big new move excited me. I had developed the ability to win others over. I loved being involved in different after-school activities. I mean, you name it, I tried it. I tried soccer. I tried basketball. I tried volleyball. These schools were so small that you could be a star player on all three teams. It was definitely a few fish in a little pond; everyone knew everyone's business. I also got into singing and acting, and on the weekends, I would tour Southern California in a sparkly red dress and sing show tunes. That didn't exactly make me cool at school, but I was finding my passion and what I loved doing. Theatrics and performing were definitely at the top of the list of things I wanted to spend more time pursuing.

When I got sent to a new high school, it gave me the idea that I could have a fresh start and be whoever I wanted to be. My parents sent me to a Dutch Christian reform school, but as an Italian with brown hair and brown eyes, I definitely stood out like a sore thumb amongst all the blonde-haired, blue-eyed Dutch kids. So, I already felt like I had a lot of work to do to win these people over and fit in.

I started making friends, and in record time, I had a boyfriend. I grew up watching *Boy Meets World*—he was just like Corey, and I thought I was Topanga. This was my life, romanticizing these situations and relationships and then trying to fit them all into the puzzle. It wasn't until we'd been dating for a year that he became what I would say was my first puppy love.

He played football, and I was a cheerleader; we had a lot of classes together, and he was very, very sweet. But we had a bad breakup. I don't remember all the details, but I do remember that I made a big mistake. Another boy had come onto the scene, and I think I cheated on him, honestly. I remember that being a big part of it. One of my girlfriends called us a "three-way," and she was one of my best friends. I remember feeling like she set me up because she called me one day and said, "Hey, Christina, I just wanted to ask you about Bobby. I heard you liked him. Did something happen with you and him?" Finally, I admitted to her that I had, indeed, kissed Bobby.

That's when my boyfriend unmuted, and I realized that I had been set up by one of my best friends. I had this horrible moment when I could not take accountability, and I felt exposed, betrayed, and sick to my stomach; I felt like nobody in the world would understand. From that moment—this was in the middle of my sophomore year—I told my parents that I did not want to go back to that school. Within the next two months, I transferred to a different school in a completely different city.

The private junior high I had attended was in Claremont, and there was a public high school there as well. Many of my junior high friends, with whom I was still close, went on to attend that public school. I begged my parents to let me go there, telling them, "I'm sick of being a big fish in a small pond. I'm ready to be a small fish in a big pond." That's a pretty dramatic thing for a four-teen-year-old to say to their parents, but I really wanted to pursue theater, and Claremont had an amazing theater program. At the end of the day, though, I could not face the hurt and the pain that I had gone through at my old school. And you know, in my mind, it happened *to* me and was something that I couldn't escape. In my mind, it was not a result of the choices that I had made. Instead, it was, *I'm following my heart; how dare anybody make me feel like I can't question anything.*

So, I made my parents switch me to a different high school. I still remember my first day on the new campus. I was the new girl who transferred in the middle of the year, so I stuck out like a sore thumb once again. I had come from a private school where girls did their full makeup and hair every single day. I mean, we're talking full glam and carrying purses instead of backpacks. When I showed up at the public school, I had—and this is no joke—little heels on. The movie *Legally Blonde* made a huge impression on me, and I really thought I was Elle Woods going to school and that I would fit right in.

At this new school, the jocks were the cool kids. Nobody did their hair and makeup for school, and everyone wore sports clothes. I remember seeing the cool kids in their area and saying,

"Those are the cool kids? Like, oh, my gosh!" To me, it was very important to identify who they were and then emulate them. I don't know if that's a product of the TV shows I grew up on, like *Saved by the Bell* and the different after-school shows, but it was very important to me to fit in—and not just in a way where I was meeting the status quo but in a way that made people notice me so that I didn't feel like I was just sort of disappearing.

So, I tried to create a new image for myself at this school because a few rumors had begun to spread because of the way I looked and walked. On my first day, I had my purse, and I was wearing flared jeans, little heels, and the wildly popular xoxo brand shirt with capped sleeves. When I walked in, I could hear the girls behind me talking about me. They very much intimidated me, and they were saying, "Look at how she walks. Look at what she's wearing. Did you hear the story about her? Did you hear what happened to her? I heard that she hooked up with a teacher. I heard that she got kicked out of her old school." No joke, it was right out of a '90s movie.

Despite being intimidated, I held my head high. Thinking back, that is really interesting to me—that even in that moment, I was like, *Okay, I'm not going to let these people see that they're getting to me.* Inside, however, I felt like my soul was being crushed and like I was dying, like, *Oh my gosh, I cannot believe these people are talking about me like this and saying these sorts of things.* Not one ounce of me wanted to turn around and correct them. I was too terrified of them.

I slowly made new friends, but I was definitely struggling with insecurity. As I was making new friends and going out, I got a new boyfriend, which was amazing for me after the heartbreak that I was getting over. Social media didn't exist back then, thank God. I don't know what I would have done if I could have opened my phone and seen my ex-boyfriend hanging out with all my old friends. I knew it was happening, and it bothered me a little, especially on the weekends—that my ex was now infiltrating my friend group—but for the most part, it was out of sight, out of mind.

I'm so grateful for that because it allowed me to move forward in my new relationships with my new friends and pursue what I thought I was going to do: musical theater. I joined the choir, but I ended up auditioning for one of the plays and not making it, and that made me really just kind of lose interest in it. It turned out that I really didn't want to pursue theater; I just thought I did. I kind of got into the party scene, and that became where I really found full-blown acceptance and comfort. When we were drinking after school or ditching class to get high or drink, I found that this was what I was looking for: that ultimate escape.

After the breakup at my old school, I had cried so hard in my room and said that I wished I didn't care. I can't tell you how many times I said that: "I wish I didn't care. I wish I didn't care. I wish I didn't care." That was before I found drugs and alcohol, which then became my way of actually not caring. I was definitely into anyone who wanted to hang out and do those things because it was my way of not caring while still feeling like I was being accepted and having friends who cared about me. That being said, even when I was partaking in the hotboxing of our cars or house parties we called "kickbacks," I was nervous about what I was doing. There was an uncertainty, but I chose to make it harder on myself and just went along with what everyone else was doing around me.

I prided myself on being outgoing and outspoken, which seemed to be one of the things that I had going for me. I ended up joining the cheer squad in my junior year at my new school. And, of course, I was the only one who got in trouble for having her cheer skirt hemmed too short. I was blossoming and developing. I had shed some baby weight and was dating one of the most popular football players. I was really finding my stride and getting a little too big for my britches, and I was in trouble quite often, but I had made really good friends. They got good grades, but they also knew how to party, and I was really enjoying that. I started letting my grades slip; it seemed like the more popular I got, the worse my grades were.

While growing up, I was called "big-boned." I don't think anybody even uses that term anymore, but that was the term used to describe me. I definitely remember one girl telling me I was "pleasantly plump" in first grade. To make matters worse, she was the new girlfriend of the boy I had a crush on. I was devastated that my little kindergarten boyfriend had a girlfriend who was calling me that.

She ended up being on my AYSO soccer team. I volunteered to be the goalie because, honestly, to me, it seemed like the best position for me to be in. I could use my hands, but I was horrible with my feet, and I couldn't jump. We were the Heat Waves, and I was really into watching *Sister Act,* so there I was on the soccer field, singing "Heat Wave" from the movie like I was in a jazz diner. The parents were shouting, "Goalie, goalie, get ready, get ready!" And I was just singing "Heat Wave." I don't even know the name of her position, but this girl was in the back with me, and I accidentally stepped on her foot. She screamed, "OW!!! You weigh a lot!" I was so utterly embarrassed by this moment that I immediately stopped playing soccer.

I told my parents, "I do not want to go back ever again." I can see now how that was a pattern for me. When I got really uncomfortable with a place, I just didn't want to go back. One day, I was sitting in the back of the car. I can't remember if we were coming home from a game or church or what we were doing, but both my parents were in the car, which was a bit of a rarity since my dad worked multiple jobs to keep us kids in private school. They were having a conversation about whether or not they should allow me to quit soccer.

I remember vividly that my dad was adamant. "No, she said she was going to do this, so she's going to see it through. We're going to have her finish it."

My mom, though, was really upset by it. "She's not going to be a soccer player. You know she's not going to do this."

I just remember hearing the debate and being like, *I'm literally right here. Like, why don't you just ask me what I want to do?* I knew that there was nothing anybody was going to be able to do to force me to continue something I didn't want to do. I was that hardheaded, strong-willed, or whatever you want to call it. However, because my emotions were so loud and strong, my embarrassment, shame, and fear were really stopping me from doing a lot.

We all experience hard things as kids. While I understand that most of my experiences were self-inflicted, there were certainly things that happened for which I didn't have a choice. I had a lot of friends with different hardships, losing their parents, losing loved ones, and having their parents get divorced—major life issues that were hard—but we can still continue to choose the same patterns into our adulthood. Ultimately, we want to be loved; we want to be listened to, and we want to be accepted. Honestly, all the quests that I set out to accomplish in my childhood were centered around those things. I wanted love. I wanted a good relationship. I wanted someone who would say, "I accept you for you. You don't even know who you are, but I accept you for you."

There's nothing that prevents you from being you other than yourself. You can try to hide yourself, change yourself, compare yourself, or have these different things about you that you want to blend in with the cool kids, or maybe you want to be an outcast. You so badly don't want to be seen as being the same as other people that you go in the polar opposite direction. Whatever it is, in a nutshell, we're all looking for the same thing. You definitely do have permission to be authentic. You have permission to be exactly what you were created to be.

We all have different strengths. We all have different skill sets. We all have different passions. We all have different gifts. I think that's why I was the show-tune-singing goalie. I think that was why I broke the window in junior high and was constantly breaking things; I was very, very accident-prone. I remember my parents saying that I would outgrow it, and I never did. I am still very accident-prone to this day.

So, instead of trying to run away from hard things, own them, and then you will see the beauty in them. It's not just about loving yourself. It's also about showing people that it's okay to have these elements and to be inspired by them. Certainly, when I was turning every single song into a show tune, I was worried about getting made fun of, even though I really enjoyed it. There were so many times when I felt like I would be happy singing something, but when someone made fun of me, the light completely disappeared, and that smile turned into a frown. That happens to so many people in so many different ways. You may not love show tunes. For you, it could be something different, something that you are excited about, but everyone around you pooh-poohs it, so you completely turned your light off.

How many of us have had that happen in our childhood in one way, shape, or form regarding something that we were so excited about? What I found is that I've continued to do that into my adult life, and it rears its head in different circumstances. But the moment when I was put in an environment where everyone was singing show tunes, I found a whole new passion and a whole new love for it. Sometimes, it's just about finding the right environment where you can thrive and be accepted for who you are and what you love.

I don't think I really ever realized that this was something that I could have requested. I mean, I knew when I wanted to get away from pain. I knew, when I was hurt in soccer, that I definitely didn't want to play soccer. When I was hurt in junior high, I never wanted to be in a bathing suit ever again, so I wore board shorts until I hit high school. So, I knew how to get away from discomfort, but I did not really know how to be drawn to the things that I was passionate about. I think that a lot of us are more geared toward running away from our fears than running toward our passions.

I think we continue that pattern into adulthood far more easily than we are drawn toward our passions and our gifts because we tend to be more reactive. We tend to be more prone to having a heightened awareness of things that make us uncomfortable, rather than the vision of knowing, *Okay, these are my strengths. These are my passions. These are the things I want to pursue.* Most people are living in defense rather than offense, and I think that's why we can find ourselves stuck in these different cycles of emotions that come with things being hard.

The emotions that I found myself repeating were guilt, shame, resentment, and feeling like I would never be enough, that I was inadequate, and that I was the black sheep, which made me people-pleasing, numbing, and constantly dealing with grief in one way, shape, or form. I was in complete defense mode. These hard emotions were a revolving door for me until I realized it and was able to identify how they had manifested in me as an adult. Most people go through their whole lives without realizing the patterns that they're repeating, and they never even put thought into dealing with their past or facing their past, because they're in such a state of getting away from things that make them uncomfortable.

We can look back as adults or young adults and say, "These are the things from my childhood." You can identify those moments just like I'll always be able to identify that junior high moment and that soccer moment when I stepped on the other girl's foot. I can remember them like they were yesterday, and I literally can't remember yesterday. We have those things that scar us, that create wounds so deep that they're unforgettable, and that can evoke an emotion.

Even writing this, my tears welled up as I recounted these moments of my life when I was that little girl who was in so much pain. And now, as an adult, I'm realizing that these same things happen. They just look a little different. Now, I'm not pointing the finger. I'm not blaming anyone, and I'm not angry with any of these people. I've forgiven. I've grown past them. I've had moments of total peace about them, even though what they did can still trigger emotions.

However, I've also identified moments in my adult life that have brought me the same exact emotions, the same exact cycles, and the same exact patterns, and I've been able to say, "Okay, I see this. This is triggered by this, so how am I going to deal with these hard emotions?" That's the only way I've been able to grow out of them and find hope in all of these hard things, not all of which are self-inflicted. As a matter of fact, once I turned a certain age, it was like I got thrown into the washing machine and put on a "tough" cycle. None of these things that happened to me were self-inflicted; they were things that there was no escaping from.

How I dealt with that was to identify them and come to peace with them. I recognized how they were affecting me and had a constant awareness of them and how I was going to deal with them. That is how I've been able to have so much hope amidst all the hard things that life has thrown my way.

In my senior year of high school, I got into beauty school through the Regional Occupational Program (ROP) at our school. This program provides career and technical education for high school students and adults. ROP programs offer hands-on training and classroom instruction to help students develop job skills.

Beauty school seemed fun. When I was eight years old, my mom had taken me to her hairstylist, and I had sat in the chair. I remember the smells, getting my hair washed, getting my hair cut, and the types of questions I asked the stylist, which were not your typical questions. They weren't really about my haircut. I asked her, "When did you know you wanted to be a hairstylist? How did you know you wanted to be a hairstylist? What was the schooling like?"

Later, when I went to beauty school and became a hairstylist, she told me, "I had a feeling you were going to be a hairstylist because you always had such a unique interest in what I did."

I made some new friends, and I made the decision to advance from marijuana to trying crystal meth for the first time. My parents were very religious, and I had done the DARE program (Drug Abuse Resistance Education). Remember, I went to private school, so I was constantly told not to do drugs and how harmful drugs were. But truthfully, the only drug that I was really told about was heroin and how, if I did it, I would end up a prostitute on the streets. I knew that I would definitely never touch that one, but the other ones, once presented to me by my peers, definitely seemed like something I wanted to experience.

I was a little heavyset, and one day, one of my new cool friends said to me, "Do you want to be really skinny?"

"Yes, I would," I replied.

"Okay, come with me after school, and we're going to go get skinny."

It was truly like a scene out of *Seventh Heaven* or *Full House*, where I was ushered into a room full of people I didn't know who definitely were from a crowd that I should not be hanging out with. However, not wanting to seem uptight, I decided to smoke crystal meth with them.

It was not anything like I'd ever imagined because drugs had been described to me as bad. I was like, *But I feel so good*. I remember going home later that day and having the best conversation I've ever had with my mom up until that point, because most of my days, I was on major defense. I was getting grilled on what I had done wrong or how I could have done better, or maybe I'd have a complete non-conversation with my mom, just tuning her out and watching TV. But with these drugs, I was extremely talkative, and I unloaded all my thoughts to my mom about work, who I was dating, and beauty school. My mom said, "If you were like this every day, we would have the best relationship."

That was when I had another aha moment: *If I can enhance myself, if I can be something other than myself, I will also have an amazing relationship with my mom*. Well, I was also getting skinny, so to me, it was a win-win. How could anybody speak horribly about this thing that was making my life so much better?

Well, we all know that the thing about drugs is that they do not make your life better. In fact, they make your life increasingly worse and harder. You become dependent on them, and if you have an addictive personality like I do, you get to a point where you build up a tolerance, so you require more and more.

A few times, I didn't sleep for days because that's what that drug does to you; you stay awake, and then you start to get super paranoid and see shadow people, and you have encounters with the devil while you do it. It's just totally the opposite of what you're created to be. You don't need to be enhanced, but I was under the impression that it was making me better—until it wasn't.

I ended up going down a path with that drug for all of my

senior year, and I never really found my footing. I started ditching class all the time. I was even ditching beauty school. Basically, I was on the brink of getting cut off from a lot. In the end, I barely graduated. My mom didn't even want to send out my high school graduation notice or announcements because we didn't even know if I was going to graduate until a couple of days before the ceremony.

I pleaded with my algebra teacher to give me a passing grade, and I promised him I would never go into math or do anything math-related. I did not think that math would have anything to do with my career. After doing all the extra credit I could, I ended up barely passing. I had a bad breakup with the guy I'd started dating sophomore year. Yup, another one. Life was just not looking good. I was definitely going nowhere fast. I was roped up with the wrong crowd and fired from one of my after-school jobs, which would end up becoming a pattern for me.

I had so much passion, but nowhere to put it, other than in places where I shouldn't. I was so focused on running away from anything that made me uncomfortable. I enrolled in a junior college to appease my parents and so I wouldn't lose my medical insurance, because I was living with them. One of the rules was that I had to have a job and go to school to stay living under their roof because I was now nineteen years old.

I'd had multiple jobs and lost them all, so I was starting to have a harder time getting new jobs because no one wanted to write me a reference from the previous job. I was also ditching school, and I had a really bad accident where I totaled my car after drinking and driving. I definitely should have gotten a DUI, but I didn't.

The accident happened while I was dating a new guy that I'd

met. He was a friend of a friend, and it was the night of my twentieth birthday, which was Halloween. My car had a flat tire, as I had run over a nail or something, so my new boyfriend of two days put my spare on. We had gone out that night to the Queen Mary in Long Beach, where they had this amazing Halloween party. I ended up saying, "I don't want to spend the night here. I'm going to drive home." But I definitely should not have driven home.

I only remember a few things from that drive home. I remember that the roads were very clear, especially for a holiday in the middle of the night. I also remember being really sleepy behind the wheel. Eventually, I fell asleep with my foot on the gas pedal as I was headed toward a brick wall. I crossed into the oncoming traffic lane and hit the curb. When I did, the tire that my new boyfriend had put on—and I don't know if this was just because it wasn't put on properly—flew off, which sent my car in the opposite direction from the brick wall that I was headed toward at probably forty to fifty miles an hour. I ended up spinning out in the middle of this road, almost under a bridge.

The oncoming traffic was coming down a hill, so if someone was drunk driving or driving really fast, they would have come right out from under that bridge and plowed right into me. To make matters worse, my cell phone had died, and I had a bottle of alcohol in the driver's seat. I remember just sitting there and saying, "I'm going to get hit." I couldn't believe what had just happened. I was in total shock, asking myself, *What happened? I was headed that way. How did I end up facing this way?* My car was tilted because my tire had come off.

The next car that came over the hill and down to me was a cop car. I felt two things. First was utter relief. I thought, *Thank God,*

I'm going to be saved, because he put on the big spotlight so drivers would notice us and not hit us. That was immediately followed by panic: *Oh, my gosh, I'm drunk, I have an open container in my car, and I'm twenty years old.*

He pulled up to me and saw that my tire had come completely off. I honestly have zero recollection of the conversation that we had. The next thing I remember is being in a tow truck and getting driven two miles up the street to my home. Once inside, I went straight into my room and went to sleep. The next morning, when I woke up, I had to face my parents and tell them what had happened. I lied and said that I'd fallen asleep at the wheel and that the spare tire had come off. I don't know if I ever told my parents what really happened, but I must have when I went through the AA program.

I could have died that night. I felt like I had a whole new lease on life, that I had been spared and was able to get out of that problem without a DUI. I had friends who had gotten DUIs and different things, but I was dabbling in drugs. My parents found out because one of my new boyfriends told them. He genuinely cared about me, and he called my parents and told them that I was doing drugs. He wanted them to know so that they could take the proper precautions. One consequence of this was that my parents pulled me out of beauty school.

I went from dabbling in drugs to getting fired from jobs to ditching school. Then, the college called to say that I was getting incompletes and wouldn't pass, which meant I would no longer be able to stay on my parents' medical insurance. My dad was already working multiple jobs to provide for what we had. There was no way that my parents were going to be able to afford my health insurance on their own. And now my car insurance was going up, too, because I'd had the accident.

I was failing junior college. I had gotten fired from my job. I was crashing cars. I was getting more expensive. I was unsafe. At this point, I was still doing at-home drug testing just to make sure that I didn't get on them again. They also put me in therapy, but I completely lied to the lady. I couldn't have cared less about actually healing in therapy, so I told her whatever I thought I needed to say. It's like I was driving, but no one was behind the wheel, if that makes sense.

My parents were at a point where enough was enough. I came home one day, and my dad was sitting at his desk. "Christy," he said, "come here." He had this little comfy chair in his office, but it had been moved so that it was right next to his desk. I sat in it, and he looked me in the eye and said, "You have no direction." He went on with a long lecture, trying to get me to understand his perspective. And then he ended it with, "Something's gotta change, and the key to life is finding what you are passionate about and then figuring out a way to get paid to do that. You seem to be very passionate about doing hair. You're even ditching school to do hair. You also seem to be passionate about being social and having friends. Why don't you go back to beauty school?" It had been about a year since my parents had pulled me out, so all the people I'd previously associated with were now gone.

The first thing I said was, "But will you be proud of me if I am just a hairstylist?"

"Oh, my gosh," he said. "Absolutely. You know, your mom's hairstylist makes more than some doctors; she probably makes more than I do. You can totally go to beauty school, and you can make a career out of it. You can take it really seriously, be very professional, and be very successful. And I'm definitely proud of you."

So, that's what I did. I feel like it changed the wind in my sails so that I stopped playing life on defense. For the first time, I was excited about life on the offense, and I began taking it seriously. I like to say I graduated from beauty school with honors. When I graduated, the whole staff, who really couldn't stand me the first time around, were saying things like, "You know, she's been such a great mentor to the new students, and she has so much potential." I was getting praised and rewarded for the efforts and the passion that I had put in, and for just really being very present while I was there. I had cleaned my act up and was going to be moving forward in life.

*** ACTION STEP ***

So, whether you don't know what you want to do in your life, or you've been down a path taken by others, or maybe you are miserable in your life and don't know what you want to do, and you know you're living life on the defense and you want to start living life on the offense, I'm going to encourage you to take some notes and write down what makes you the happiest. Then, write down when you are the happiest. Give yourself a few moments to really identify those things because if you want to start playing life on the offense and stop playing defense, you have to stop looking at what makes you run away from things and instead focus on what you want to run toward.

I'm so grateful for the conversation that my dad had with me in which he woke me up from the haze of life that I was living in, with no direction, purpose, or passion, and had me focus on what I wanted. This made me grow a vision of the joy that my life would have if I achieved these things. Now, I had a whole new goal, a whole new focus, and it was a total game changer for **hope** in my life. So, if you don't have someone to have that conversation with, let it be me right here, right now: "What are **you** passionate about?" I'm going to encourage you to take a few moments for yourself today and think about what makes you the happiest. When are you the happiest? What are you most passionate about? Give yourself some time to really think about this; look at your calendar right now and schedule something in there.

If you aren't sure how you can, plan some time to explore ways or resources. You can get in touch with someone who can point you in the right direction. For example, if it has to do with volunteer work at the hospital or senior living home, it's easy to say, "I don't know how to get involved," and throw it on the back burner. This book is to drive you into action steps, so pick up your phone and figure it out, girlfriend. Make it a priority.

CHAPTER Two

GRIEF

I lost a cat and my two grandpas in my life, but my first true experience with grief happened shortly after I turned twenty-eight. My entire past and its hardships were behind me. My husband and I were celebrating one year of wedded bliss, and my life and career were looking good. Josh and I had secretly started to try for a baby, and we were looking to buy our first home. Everything was so good.

I was also in my first big season of doing hair behind the chair during the holidays, which in the salon world is like the Super Bowl of hair seasons. So, it was a really exciting time, and I was loving life. I would come home from work, we would cook dinner, have some wine, and watch TV. When I was in the thick of it, I would turn off my phone notifications, as I needed a full night's sleep, but clients would text at all hours of the night, asking to get squeezed in for the holidays, which is a great problem to have when you are growing a thriving clientele and business as a hairstylist.

The Monday before Thanksgiving, our one-year-old dog, Sherlock, woke us up in the middle of the night, barking like crazy. He ran to our front door and let out a series of the deepest, loudest barks we'd ever heard from him, as though an intruder were trying to break into our apartment.

We got out of bed, and I stood behind my husband because I grew up watching *Dateline* and legitimately thought, *This is it; the boogeyman is here.* But when he looked through the peephole, he saw that it was one of our family friends, and she looked really disheveled, like maybe she had been crying. Then I thought, *Oh, she probably had a bad breakup and is drunk.* With a sigh of relief, I opened the door.

I opened the door, and right when I was about to ask, "What are you doing here?" she blurted out, "Your dad has been in a horrible motorcycle accident, and he was airlifted to a hospital."

It was like time stood still. I took a few steps back and sort of gestured for her to come in. The only words that I could speak were, "Is he alive?"

"I'm not sure," she said. "I'm not sure."

I ran to my phone and saw a bunch of missed calls and text messages from my mom. After failing to reach me, she knew that the best thing to get my attention was to call my friend, because she lived down the street, while I lived about an hour from my parents.

I called my mom, and she said, "I'm at the hospital with your aunt and uncle. He's been in a horrible accident, and we don't know all the injuries, but he's in bad shape. He's alive, but it doesn't look good. He was hit on his motorcycle on his way home from work."

After I hung up, my husband and I left immediately for the hospital. I had never experienced a phone call like that, a visit like that, or news like that, so I just instinctively grabbed my car keys and headed for the car—so quickly that I almost forgot my shoes.

I put on my shoes, and then Josh and I got in the car, and we drove a little over an hour north from Newport to the USC Medical Center. The whole way there, it was a little drizzly, and I could only think, *No way. There's no way that my dad could be dying or taken or gone. I can't live without him. He's going to be okay. He has to be okay.* I even prayed that he just had a broken neck. You hear stories like that all the time, and I didn't know any details. I just knew what my mom had told me.

When we arrived at the hospital, we parked and then walked across a bridge and rode up an elevator. As soon as we got into the cold hospital, the sun was starting to rise. My mom was in the waiting room with my uncle and aunt, just sitting there. The moment we walked into the room, we turned around, and my dad was getting wheeled by. They had taken him somewhere for X-rays or some testing, and they were wheeling him back into the ICU. He looked like he was sleeping, but his entire body was bruised and a bit bloody, and I realized just how serious this was. I thought, *Oh, my gosh. I don't know if he's going to make it.*

I had no idea what to expect, but he ended up spending the next four weeks in a coma at that hospital. Lots of very interesting things happened through my grief journey with him in the hospital. If you've never had a loved one in a coma, let me just tell you, seconds feel like hours, and hours feel like days. Time moves extremely slowly because, every single second, you're waiting for your loved one to wake up or for the doctors to tell you if they are going to live or die. As for my dad, the doctors informed us that he had suffered such a traumatic brain injury that even if he were to wake up, he would have a very low quality of life. There was one nurse who would repeatedly tell us, "This is a life-changing injury," which ended up being the most accurate statement of my life if there ever was one.

I remember one of my parents' friends coming in at the end of the first week that my dad was in the hospital and saying, "I just can't believe what he said on the air."

"What do you mean?" I asked. "What did he say on the air?"

Dad had a Christian radio talk show that broadcast Monday through Friday in L.A. from 4 to 7 p.m., making it the prime drive-time talk show. Not to brag, but really, yes, I'm bragging, lol. I am a proud daughter. He won awards and received national recognition for his show, which is unheard of for a local LA show. He had the largest audience of any Christian talk show in America. His accident was on a Monday, and that day, he had been talking about the book *Proof of Heaven*, which is about a neurosurgeon who was in a coma and visited Heaven. He talked with Dr. Keith Matthews from Azusa Pacific University about the reality of our soul and said—and this is an exact quote—"Look, you all know I ride a motorcycle, right? At any moment, I could be spread all over the 210 Freeway because of the idiot drivers that, you know, pull into the diamond lane, my lane. They could, someone could hit me, and I could be all over the 210, but that's not me; that's my body parts."

Three hours later, he was driving home on the 210, and a

drowsy driver, who ended up being a nurse coming off of her shift who had actually listened to his radio show, veered into the diamond lane and struck him, and he had to be resuscitated at the scene and then airlifted to the hospital.

When I heard what he'd said, I just knew he was not going to be waking up. For his story to have an impact, he would need to not wake up. He would need to be a soul that was no longer here —just his body parts. It's unreal how there was so much peace in that. It was almost like he knew what would happen. This brought me peace, even though it was the biggest heartbreak I had ever been through.

I didn't go to work for those first two weeks. I was just at the hospital. I wanted to be there when he woke up and opened his eyes. I also wanted to be there to support my mom, with whom, at that point, I didn't have the best relationship. As a matter of fact, we had just gone to lunch with girlfriends a few days before the accident. My mom and I were notorious for getting into fights in front of other people, having arguments over dumb things, and making other people at the table uncomfortable. We would even bring other people into some of our arguments. After this particular lunch, we called off the holidays because of the fight that we'd gotten into about my childhood cat and how he died. I mean, we really got into the dumbest debates.

However, after my dad's accident, we said, "Let's put all the petty stuff behind us," and I just really wanted to be there to support her and spend time with her because my mom married my dad when she was sixteen years old, and they got together when she was thirteen, so she had never lived without him or dealt with anything like this. It was truly a life-changing accident.

After a few weeks, the bills piled up, and I had to get back to work. So, I would work every single day and just sob. All my clients would want to hear updates and hear the story. Word had gotten around about what my dad had said on his radio show, and a lot of people wanted to talk about that, too.

I thought that I was way too fragile a human being to handle the situation. I was such a daddy's girl. I was certain that it would break me. I mean, little things made me want to escape life. This was the first big thing that I had ever faced, and I wanted so badly to wake up from the nightmare.

Sometimes, I would wake up with a wet pillow, and my husband would say, "You were doing it again."

"Doing what?" I'd ask.

"Crying in your sleep," he'd reply.

I had no idea that you could be so heartbroken or grieving so deeply that you actually wept in your sleep, but that's how hard my body was taking it. At this point, we had been trying to get pregnant for about six months. I just knew that the trauma of all of this was not going to make it any more likely that I would be getting pregnant anytime soon.

After my dad passed away, I was in the middle of my workday, and my mom's sister called me and said that my dad had passed away right after our pastor visited him. It was amazing that it happened the way that it did because we had gotten to the point where he was getting moved out of the ICU and into a rehab center. They'd told us that my mom was going to have to make some decisions because, in my dad's directives (directives are in your will), he'd said that he did not want to be kept alive by extraordinary means, and the situation was getting to that point.

They had tested his heart, and he was eating multiple bags of food a day through a feeding tube. He had a really big appetite. Here's a fun tangent and side story to break up the sad one I'm telling you right now: So, there's this restaurant called The Big Texan in Amarillo, TX, and they have a 72-ounce steak on the menu that is the size of a telephone book. If you eat it in an hour or less, it's free. If you become ill, you lose—they literally provide a bucket.

There are all these rules, and it caught my dad's attention because he had a big appetite and a competitive nature. Well, he ended up completing it seven separate times. The first time, in 1976, he completed it in 21 minutes. Then he got it down to 19 minutes, then 17 minutes, then 15 minutes, then 13 minutes, and then 11 minutes, and he held the world record for decades with his 9.5 minutes in 1987. He was dethroned in 2008 by a professional eater who did it in 8:52. My dad is still the fastest amateur eater to ever complete the challenge. Oddly, I take great pride in this fact.

Okay, back to my grief. This is exactly how grief works, though—you feel it, then you forget it for a moment, and then you feel it again.

We found a way to laugh about how much his body ate while he was in a coma. Despite how healthy his body seemed to be, his brain was not working properly, so we prayed that the Lord would take him. It's such a strange thing to make the switch from praying for a miracle and for him to wake up to praying for him to pass away. After our pastor visited, my dad ended up having a cardiac arrest. I felt like it was a gift that he was no longer going to be in pain, but the loss of my dad was the biggest, hardest thing that I'd ever had to face. Little did I know that it was just the beginning of the most transformative year of my life.

While I was grieving my dad, the only thing that I had to compare to the emotions I was feeling was heartbreak. I have shared about my heartbreak before, but my first real heartbreak happened like this. The guy I lost my virginity to broke my heart in a horrible, gut-wrenching way. I cried and felt sick for weeks, and I really thought that that was it for me. I was young and obviously naïve, but I really believed that he was the man I would spend the rest of my life with at the very mature and seasoned age of seventeen years old.

I was the new girl on campus, and as I started to make friends, I definitely developed crushes on a guy or two. I had never been in a world as big as this one. It felt like a college campus from the movies, and I was **so young**. I knew I was going to be auditioning to be a cheerleader my junior year, and one of the football players in my grade caught my attention because he was one of the funniest guys on campus, always into practical jokes, and he seemed to always be involved in whatever shenanigans or pranks were going down at school. He had a girlfriend who was a year older than us, which intrigued me. He definitely had a reputation, but I was a "learn for myself" type of girl and down for a challenge.

It started with some group dates to do seriously romantic things like going to the county fair. Now, if you've watched any rom-com from the '90s, you know exactly what I'm talking about: holding hands, riding rides, going to Sadie Hawkins dances in matching outfits, movie dates, long walks on the beach, and staying up late on the phone and talking for hours. It was textbook first-love vibes, something that I had never experienced before. He charmed my parents, he charmed my friends, and he charmed his way into my soul. I let my emotions make my decisions for me, and as "unchristian" as it is—that's the way my story goes—I know it made the breakup a hundred times harder.

We dated for a few amazing months and were seriously one of the cutest couples—like Faith Hill and Tim McGraw. If you have ever seen *Varsity Blues*, I felt like I was living that movie. He got all of the cheerleaders in on it when he asked me to homecoming. This was the 2000s, okay? Not everyone asked in a fancy way, but he did. I was a base in our cheerleading stunts, but on this night, the girls said, "Tina, you're gonna fly!" I didn't ask any questions at all; I just did what the girls said. They lifted me up into the stunt, and then my girlfriend spoke into her megaphone, "The crowd has a question they want to ask you, Tina." They spun me around, and there it was—the *"Will you go to homecoming with me?"* signs. Talk about sweeping a girl off her feet! To someone who thought a kiss in the rain was romantic, this was off the charts! So things were great until they weren't. As the saying goes, "Players gonna play."

When he broke up with me, he told me that he wished we had met later in life because I would be someone he saw himself marrying, but that he honestly just wanted to experience more things before he settled down. Then he said the infamous words, **"I just want to be friends."** FRIENDS?! Those words literally ripped my heart right out of my chest. I can remember the devastation and sick-to-my-stomach feeling so vividly (cue: breakup diet). But I was just hung up on him, and I would take him in any way I could. So I asked if we could be friends with benefits. Ten out of ten do not recommend this; this is clearly an act from an emotionally unstable person who is trying to remain in an unhealthy attachment, an indicator of how insecure and emotionally immature I was.

A week later, word blasted through school that he'd asked one of the hottest chicks on the dance team from a younger class to the upcoming school dance on the radio. Really? The radio? I think it was K-Frog, and I'm pretty sure I refused to listen to that station for years afterward. (For the record: I ended up being friends with all the girls mentioned in this story and adore them still to this day. He and I became friends in later years, and I truly wish him and his family the best.)

Um, where was I? Back to my heartbreak. See? There are the waves of grief again.

I had spent multiple days in a row crying on my bed. I couldn't eat. I couldn't sleep. I mean, I was truly heartbroken, devastated. It took a physical toll on me, and I felt like I had no control over my emotions and my grief.

One day, I had been weeping loudly for several hours when I heard a gentle knock at my door.

"Come in," I said between sobs.

My dad pushed the door open and stood there, crying. "I can't take you crying anymore," he said. "I wish there was something I could do."

Then he lay on the bed and cried with me. He was just the best dad.

I just wanted to escape those feelings, and I prayed to stop caring and for the heartache to go away. I couldn't change schools again because I had already switched after the last puppy-love breakup, and this breakup seemed so much more colossal and monumental. I just knew that I would have to face the situation this time and get through it, and not run away.

So, the only thing I could compare the loss of my dad to was that bad breakup I had been through, where there was no waking up from the bad dream; you just had to get up and face it every single day. But how do you get up every single day when you're struggling with grief?

The way I did it was knowing that I was going to be in pain, but realizing that I had responsibilities and things that I had to do. It was my first time as an adult knowing I had clients to tend to. I had a dog to take care of and a husband to look out for. I had real-life things to deal with; I couldn't just lie on my bed and cry for hours and let my emotions take over and not eat, not take care of myself, not do anything, and bring other people down with me. I had to put one foot in front of the other, wake up every single day, and get things done.

Laughter and joy are also parts of medicine, so I allowed myself to laugh and get lost in things like movies or hanging out with friends. When you're suffering from acute grief, you can still be taken for a moment by something and forget, and it feels like a mini-vacation for your brain because you're actually able to allow that grieving pain to subside. Eventually, you think, *Wait. Why is it hard to breathe?* Then you remember, *Oh, yeah. My dad died, and I'm grieving.* Just knowing that you're going to be on that ride and not trying to completely run away from it is the first step to getting through it.

In the stage of grief where you're negotiating, you can renegotiate relationships, the things that you're doing in your life, or your patterns. Basically, you're asking yourself, *What's more important? What do I care about? What matters to me?* Part of your grief is re-evaluating almost every single thing in your life. *Why do I care about this? This doesn't matter. This, though, is really important to me.* You're prioritizing and sorting through everything. Every relationship, every event, and every decision.

It's very easy to say, "I can't allow myself to forget this pain because the moment I remember it, it will hit me all over again, and I will have to relive everything." A part of me wanted to try that, thinking, *I don't want to forget because then I'll remember, and the remembering is so hard and painful that it's like it's happening all over again.*

But there's another thing that happens when you want to just completely escape and go into denial: You prioritize the pain so low that it's almost like nothing happened. You've probably been around someone who's done this. They don't want to talk about it. They don't want to face it. They don't want to go to the hospital. They don't want to attend the funeral. They don't want to acknowledge it. They don't want to post about it. There's a total avoidance. And while there's no wrong type of grief, especially while things are still happening, I definitely feel like I wanted to try all the ways, and I'm actually genuinely shocked by the fact that I didn't go into denial about it, considering my history of complete and utter avoidance of hard things.

What I will say is that I was drinking wine every day by 3 or 4 p.m. because I really, really, really wanted to numb that pain. While I couldn't get rid of it completely, I definitely found a way to numb it, and every single morning, I would wake up and get re-hit with the grief, the reality that we had been dealt. But every single day, sometimes by four, the first bottle of wine would get cracked open, and sometimes, a second would be cracked open, and sometimes, it would be me all by myself. I really never consciously thought about "healthy" grieving, but I knew I was surviving the day by any means necessary. Lately, I have not been numbing so much, and I often think about the patterns in my life that I was just repeating, that cycle of, *Okay, I'm feeling something uncomfortable. I'm going to run away from it or get it to where I'm not feeling that pain anymore.* It reminds me of that fifteen-year-old girl who was going through that heartbreak and just praying not to care.

But there I was at twenty-eight, praying for the exact same thing—not to care. This time, it just came in the form of a wine bottle. What truly helped me through my grief was realizing that there is a proper and healthy way to grieve. While I had done it half right in the first few years, I was still going to be carrying the trauma of everything yet to come in my life.

Years later, I ended up going to therapy and dealing with all the underlying issues, connecting the dots between what I was going through then and what I had gone through in my childhood, and creating an awareness of how they correlated. I hadn't done that before, although reading it probably makes a lot of sense: *Oh, yeah, okay, that's how you're wired. That's what you're predisposed to feel. That's what you're used to going through.* Grief can feel like utter chaos in your life if you're not dealing with it healthfully and going through the steps of writing down your emotions and being aware of them so that you're not simply repeating the same unhealthy cycle.

*** ACTION STEP ***

My action step for you at the end of this chapter on grief is to seek counseling, whether it's with a therapist or simply talking with a friend or loved one. If you feel like you don't have anyone you can talk to, write it down in a journal. One of the most impactful things I did in therapy years after my dad died was recounting step by step every single emotion that I experienced while he was in the hospital and in the relationship I had with my mom. Gosh, was it painful, and it would have been easier to avoid it all, but facing it is the only way through it.

If I had done this at the time, I would have focused on the following questions: *Why am I numbing myself? Why am I wired to numb? Why do I have this desire? I've had friends who have lost loved ones, and they did not turn to that, so why do I? What emotions arise? What aspects of my life will need to change? Who will it affect and how? Why is this important to me?*

So, wait until you can be alone with your thoughts. Then take a few moments, maybe the rest of the day, to put pen to paper and write down the things that you're grieving, the emotions that accompany that grief, and why. Take a deep breath and know there is hope.

CHAPTER *Three*

HUMOR AS A HIDING PLACE

I was in full swing, working in the salon. I had built up a substantial clientele and was becoming a major financial contributor to our household. Living in Southern California is really expensive, so I booked clients back to back to back to back. I didn't even schedule time to use the restroom or eat, because time = money.

Josh and I were still grieving the loss of my dad. We didn't have a funeral for him, but my mom wanted a "Celebration of Life," which was at the end of December, so it felt like the turning of a page into a new chapter. It was maybe a week after the service that I turned to Josh and said, "I need joy now. I need a baby now." Trying to conceive was enough to send me down a spiraling path of darkness. Anybody who has struggled to conceive knows what it's like: You live your life in two-week increments. I went from the quest to find love and a husband to the quest to have a baby, and I was completely taken with the obsession.

Paired with grieving the loss of my dad, I immediately knew that whatever I had to do to get a baby, I was going to do it. So, I went to the first round of fertility testing. We had had quite a few friends who struggled to get pregnant and even some friends who had already adopted, so I had a little inkling that this could potentially be our reality. About a week after my first appointment, they called me with my results. I was working back-to-back clients; burying myself in work was what got me through. I rarely took any days off, and work became what I did to deal with the fact of how out of control I felt with everything going on and all the pain and question marks in the air. I will never forget the day that I got the call to tell me my first round of results. I was extremely anxious as I took each client because I knew that I could get the call at any time.

The first thing the person on the line said was, "Hi, Christina. Unfortunately, I have some hard news. Maybe you would like to sit down." At that point, I was already outside the salon, leaning up against the stucco wall and letting my body completely slide all the way to the ground. I thought, *I'm going to sit down*. My head was in my hands, and I held the phone up next to my ear, and she said, "You have extremely low AMH levels. You have what's called diminished ovarian reserve, which means we probably want to start talking about IVF and fertility treatments. And if you do happen to get pregnant naturally, it's very likely that it won't be viable, and you'll miscarry."

Time sort of stood still. I was still grieving my dad, and now this devastating news. I just remember thinking, *Okay, that's out.* Not even an ounce of me thought, *I'm going to get pregnant. I'm going to try. We're going to do IVF.*

I kept working because I had a full stack of clients that day, but I had a really hard time holding anything in. I know some people can receive news and not divulge it to their clients, but I had a very open relationship with all of mine. So, every single person who sat in that seat could see the pain, worry, and grief on my face. They all just thought I was still grieving my dad.

Each one of them asked, "Is it your dad?"

"No," I would reply. I just got the news that I'm probably not going to be having a baby."

They all responded with this question, "What did Josh say?"

And that's when I'd get nervous, thinking, *Oh my gosh, my husband just saw the worst of me as I was grieving my dad, and now I have to tell him about this? What is Josh going to say?* The whole way home from the salon to our apartment, I practiced what I was going to say. None of that actually ended up helping me because the moment I saw him, I just started crying.

"What's wrong?" he asked.

"I spoke to the fertility place today," I replied, "and they said I have low AMH, whatever that means. They said I have this thing called diminished ovarian reserve and that it's unlikely that I am able to conceive. Like, we're not going to have a baby by me."

It's weird that I said it like that, but I just blurted it all out. Then the thought hit me like a ton of bricks: What if he is not down with this? People get separated over this all the time. *Oh my gosh, I am broken, and now I'm going to be the reason my husband wants a divorce.* After a few minutes of my mind racing and the tears flowing, I blurted out, "Do you still want to be married to me?" I held my breath as I waited for his response because I had just put this man through the wringer, crying every single day, emotionally distraught, and absent a lot of the time because I was with my mom, and now we'd received more life-changing, sad news.

He just said, "What am I, a medieval king? Bear a child for me or be banished from the kingdom? Dude, it's fine. We will adopt."

When we were dating, we told one another that we were both open to adoption one day. I kind of felt like that was just something a lot of people said, like, "Oh, yeah, I'd be open to it." But to actually be living a reality where you are now faced with the decision, that's a whole other ballgame—one that apparently we were going to play.

I had not really grieved properly over my dad, and with this layer added to the pain, I was quick to want to move on, especially given my numbing tendency. I said, "Okay, I'm going to give myself twenty-four hours, the rest of the night, to have one big pity party for myself. I'm going to cry and be really sad, and then after that, I'm not grieving this anymore. Then, I'm moving forward with a plan. I'm going to do something." I just kind of numbed myself to the grief. My body had failed me in something that I really wanted and that I'd tried for over a year to do. I didn't properly grieve any of that. Instead, I moved immediately into thinking about adoption.

Today, I have zero regrets about this. God knew what was coming in our story.

Coincidentally, my mom was still dealing with all the widow things that involved finances, insurance, and paperwork, and she had recently had an appointment with their trust attorney. She told me that she'd had a meeting with him and that he randomly went on a tangent about his true passion, adoptions. She was at the appointment with my brother and his pregnant wife, so it was interesting that he went on and on about the adoptions. He had adopted multiple children and was one of the top adoption attorneys in the state.

Looking back, obviously, I know that the Holy Spirit put it on his heart to share with them that day. That was actually one of the first things my mom told me about after I told her what the fertility clinic said about my results.

I thought, *Okay, my dad sort of brought me this opportunity to meet this amazing adoption attorney in the state of California, and my mom is connected to him because of the loss of my dad. So that's who I'm going to be reaching out to next week.*

I got right on the phone and made an appointment—it felt like a breath of fresh air, like I finally stepped onto an escalator after being stranded on static ground. People often ask me if I've ever had a miscarriage, and I don't believe that I have, but I'm not one hundred percent certain.

There was one time, and one time only, that I saw those two pink lines on a pink dye pregnancy test. I was never so pumped in my life, and I ran all around my girlfriend's house screaming and crying tears of joy. We were doing hair and makeup on a close client of ours, and I showed them to confirm that my eyes weren't just seeing things—they saw the two faint lines, too. I carried pregnancy and ovulation sticks with me everywhere. I made an appointment to get my blood tested the next day, and a few days later, they called and confirmed I was not pregnant.

Later, I discovered there's a website called Pink Dyes Are the Devil because, if you're ever going to have a chance of getting a false positive, it's most likely from a pink dye pregnancy test. At the time, though, I was really excited, and I didn't let that bummer stop me from moving forward. I began to really plan ahead and thought, *I need to have pregnancy announcement photos. That way, I don't even need to wait a second before I tell Josh when I get pregnant.*

So, I took pregnancy announcement pictures. I had a cute little apron on, my hair and makeup were done, and I was in my girlfriend's kitchen, taking a cinnamon bun out of the oven and smiling happily. I had them printed out—back then, every picture you took would be printed out because you'd taken it with a camera, not your phone—I had them in a box ready to go. So after our infertility news, and we started the adoption process, I just thought, *These are cute pictures of my journey. I'll tell a story with them one day.*

I continued to numb myself. When you're going through infertility, people will give you lots of advice, and I heard it all. I think that with the trauma of everything with my dad and truly grieving, I just sort of told myself, *I don't even want to mess with getting my hopes up and something happening where I'm going to have to face another hardship.* So, the way I instinctively numbed was actually through avoidance. I thought, *I'm not even going to allow myself to hope for this because it's just not in the cards for me, and I can't even deal with the pain that could happen with it.*

I told jokes constantly. I also discovered that journaling was a way to get my feelings out there. I realized when my dad was in the hospital that I did not enjoy people pitying me at all. I actually despise being pitied or anyone feeling sorry for me in any way. My first major rejection was getting made fun of publicly by my crush when I was in junior high, and I turned to humor to cope with it.

That was my way of getting through. You've seen people respond, "You're so funny"? "Thanks, it's because of my childhood trauma."

I started an Instagram account called "Bunless Oven." With this account, I intended to document my journey of infertility, which was essentially just our adoption prep. I knew that I had this way of sort of getting ahead of anyone pitying me or feeling sorry for me. Also, when I googled "diminished ovarian reserve," I couldn't find anybody else who had it, so I thought the account was a great way to create some sort of awareness or connect with other people who were possibly going through the same thing.

However, when I posted things, instead of them being very serious, I would make light of the situation. I found that humor was really my way of numbing myself. So, instead of journaling and keeping it to myself, I would sort of journal and not allow myself to feel the pain. I was spinning everything with this very toxic-positivity vibe. I just couldn't be real with myself about the pain, which was sort of similar to the pain I'd felt when I was in junior high.

Along the same lines, there's one other event that molded me into a person who feared being embarrassed and hated uncomfortable emotions. It happened when I was in junior high, and there was a boy that I really liked. I made sure everybody knew it because I thought that if I told everybody, someone would tell him, and that once he knew that, he'd want to *go out* with me.

I was a bit of a strong-willed kid and really thought that I could make things happen with my words. Now, at the time, you have to remember that I was a "pleasantly plump" and "sassy gal." At our school, we had a big outdoor swimming pool. It reminded me of something in a summer camp show because you had to walk through a little woodsy area to get to it.

One day, I was at one end of the pool, and my crush was on the other side. I was wearing this Roxy one-piece that was kind of like from the '40s. It was a very modest suit, with little shorts attached, and it was mostly black but with white piping down the sides. As I was swimming, I heard him yelling from across the pool, "Is that Shamu? Look, a beached whale!" I wanted to run away, but that would have involved me getting out of the water to get my towel and everybody staring at me, and I was already very embarrassed. I was the girl who would wear her towel all the way to the edge of the pool and then set it down and get right in the water so no one could see my back or front. To make matters worse, someone had moved my towel.

Instead of running away, because I couldn't at that moment, I thought *I need to make this comfortable*. So, I just threw my body out of the water, arched my back, and stretched my arms up the way Shamu would when she came out of the water with her back and front fins up. And I laughed, and I laughed, and I laughed, and that was really where my ability to use comedy as a way of escaping was developed. My friends laughed, too. Some of them didn't hear what my crush said, but they enjoyed my little "Free Willy" act, and I just played it off. I remember crying as I got dressed that day and hating the way I looked. I remember being so unhappy with my body, my hair, and even though I was wearing a cool brand, it wasn't new or like what the other girls were wearing. I felt trapped in my body, and it was somewhere I did not want to be. Of course, looking back now, I just see an adorable little girl, but I remember it felt like the only thing that existed was my suffering. Being a mother to daughters, knowing how **big** these emotions can be is so eye-opening. In a way, it makes me feel like I just need to parent my girls like they are "little Christinas."

I think about that almost every single time I'm in a pool, and it has stayed with me my entire life. I'm sure there are bits and pieces of it that rear their head in different moments when I am embarrassed, like when I say the wrong thing or something doesn't go the way I wanted it to, and I really have learned to use humor as a coping mechanism.

I was definitely hurt by these moments—like the girl in first grade who told me I weighed a lot after I accidentally stepped on her foot. Or the time I made the decision to cheat on my boyfriend, and everyone found out, putting me on blast during a three-way call. Feeling triggered, I was able to escape by essentially running away to a new school.

Over time, I developed a pattern of escaping the different emotions that come from hard things. Whether it was me choosing these things or just being a product of the environment I was in, I remember thinking that life would always be hard and that life would always have challenges. Once I developed my use of humor and then discovered alcohol and marijuana as other ways to escape, I found that I could have pockets of comfort throughout those moments of life when I just wanted to run away or change them. Instead of facing things head-on and accepting a challenge or accountability at all, I turned to what a lot of people turn to—comfort zones.

My biggest takeaway for anyone who is facing any kind of life-changing or life-altering diagnosis is that these words do not define you and your value as a human being. Dealing with them, facing them, identifying them, and not letting them have complete power over your emotions is really important. Someone you love might end up getting diagnosed with something, so it's vital that you feel and ride the waves and be empathetic. But if you can't even be empathetic with yourself, or maybe the polar opposite, where you're so overly emotional about it that you let it rule you and completely change everything about the course of action you will be taking, it can derail your life.

I was not the person with an infertility diagnosis who wanted to avoid baby showers, who said, "Why not me?" when I saw all my other friends getting pregnant. My first inkling, in fact, that I might have an issue with having a baby was when I started trying to conceive with a few girlfriends. We had all gotten married around the same time, and so we all tried to get pregnant around the same time. Then, at some point, I was holding their babies and going to multiple baby showers. I remember asking, "When's it gonna happen for me?" But once I got that diagnosis, I could put a name to what I was experiencing. It was almost like I could get a little bit of breath in my lungs. Though the news was earth-shattering, now I could create a new plan of action. I know so many women who struggle with this; I believe the numbers for infertility in 2024 are insane.

They're astronomical.

It's more common now than it ever was when I was first diagnosed, and my heart goes out to the many women who are suffering from and struggling with infertility. But there are so many other things that also relate to this. You could be waiting for a promotion. You could be waiting for him to propose. You could be waiting for the call for your diagnosis. You could be putting your life on pause for all kinds of things.

One of the best leadership tips I got was from author and pastor John Maxwell, who said that you need to learn to sit before you can learn to stand. To me, he was talking about not being reactive. So, it's interesting that while I tended to want to be numb, I would give myself twenty-four hours, although that's not an appropriate amount of time at all, to properly grieve something. I did have the instinct to say, "Okay, I'm gonna allow myself this before I make a decision." I believe that it's important to give yourself an appropriate amount of time to allow yourself to feel before you make decisions. I know I'm probably on the more extreme side of the scale when it comes to impatience, and this was particularly true given the circumstances and the level of grieving I was experiencing. I definitely feel that I was more inclined to want to rush out of that pain and get that numbness going.

There's no avoiding things in life. We all create habits and patterns. Whatever it is that you're not doing, you're choosing. And while I am so happy with the way that my life turned out, numbing yourself, escaping, and running away from things just does not help any kind of situation. It also doesn't allow room for you to have the proper conversations and relationships that you need. Had my husband wanted to have more conversations about adopting or hadn't agreed to take that route, I don't know what would have happened because I had such a strong need to move forward quickly just to be numb to what I was feeling and to escape it.

People would always say to me that it was so noble that we were doing this charitable act, but in my mind, it was the fastest way to grow my family. So, I didn't really love anyone saying things like that to me, as it was out of unhealthiness that I was so adamantly pursuing this quest of adoption.

I think that's just a testament to the fact that everyone is going through something, and you have no idea from the outside looking in of the multitude of emotions that accompany someone's hardship. Even if it is a back-to-back type of grieving, especially when it comes to a diagnosis of any kind, it's going to feel like a whirlwind. There are going to be days when you feel like it's not a problem, and then, from out of nowhere, there will be days when you feel like you can't escape it. Just as I couldn't escape getting made fun of publicly and laughing about it, I could not escape this diagnosis that I was now facing.

*** ACTION STEP ***

If you feel like you are going through something or you're waiting for something, whether it's a diagnosis, a promotion, your partner to propose, or whatever, I would love for you to audit your day, your week, and the things that you are avoiding. Do you shop? Do you drink excessively? Ask yourself why you're doing that. Ask yourself what kind of pain you might be avoiding or what serious thing you might be trying to make less severe. Then, determine if you're leaving unresolved feelings on the table. I will share with you that years after becoming a mom, it hit me that I had never grieved the loss of my ability to bear children. When I actually sat with those emotions years later, I went through the stages of grief.

I was so happy. I think that sometimes you can be fearful of grieving as an adoptive parent because you might think that you're not grateful for what you have or that you love your child less than you should. But eventually, I did properly grieve my body's inability to have children, and I allowed myself to feel all the emotions.

I remember talking about it to my girlfriends and other women who went through the same thing. I believe that it's very important to allow yourself to visit these places of emotion with others who have also experienced the same things and made it through to the other side. I have related to women and talked with ones who had adopted, ones who went through IVF, ones who had miscarriages, and ones who never had children.

One key to developing hope from your situation is that you don't live there. You don't move in and stay there. Avoidance can trick you into believing that you've moved on, and while it seems like you don't live there anymore, you realize you were just asleep and dreaming in that sad house when you wake up.

You could have gone through something in the past that you have yet to deal with, or you could be going through something right now that you'd rather do anything than think about or talk about. My action step for you is that the next time you catch yourself avoiding pain or making light of something that hurts you, get out a paper and pen, and at the top of the paper, title it the painful thing you're avoiding. Brain dump whatever thoughts come to you, and then say a prayer over it. Then, I want you to stand up and do ten jumping jacks. Author and motivational speaker Tony Robbins teaches that you can change your habits by changing your state of mind. So, when you catch yourself running away from yourself or avoiding your true emotions, you can physically change your state of mind by doing something like jumping jacks.

By associating *avoidance* with a new action and getting your body moving, you can actually get yourself into a new habit. Awareness is great. Identifying your pain point is half the battle. I do not want you to move in and live with those hard feelings (although at first it may feel like it takes the wind right out of your sails). You've got to face them head-on and allow yourself to feel them—but the whole point is for you to realize they should not have power over you. Remind yourself this is not permanent; it's temporary. Now, instead of a hopeless day avoiding everything on repeat, you're going to have hopeful days ahead just by switching your steps.

CHAPTER *Four*

INADEQUACY

Two things happen when you start telling people that you are going to adopt a child. First, people begin to look at you as if to say, "Oh, wow, that's awesome." This is almost immediately followed by, "Oh, something really sad probably happened to you."

As someone who has harbored feelings of inadequacy since I was young and faced so many rejections, I couldn't handle this reaction most of the time. So, I found myself not wanting to tell people, which was difficult for me given the number of clients I had, the open relationships I had with them, and how often we were conversing. I had a new person in my chair about every two hours, so there were a lot of conversations. I found that some days, I didn't even want to talk about it because I just couldn't handle it; it was a reminder of the inadequacy that I was experiencing, though I was extremely excited to be in the adoption process.

For us, the process was actually pretty wild. I guess that's not that surprising, considering the turn our lives had taken just a few months before. On our wedding anniversary, I was very happy that we had made it another year and that we seemed to be closer than ever because of everything we had been through. We had gotten news that we were able to buy our first home, so we were celebrating that.

I built a nursery, though maybe that was part of my unhealthy coping or moving forward in my life without really facing the hardships. However, I felt it was kind of like a *Field of Dreams* thing: "If you build it, (they) will come," and that by building it, we would be blessed with a baby sooner rather than later.

Our anniversary falls around Father's Day, the same weekend every year, and I had gotten Josh a Father's Day card from our unborn, who-knows-where-they're-coming-from baby. That was also my way of avoiding the pain of my first Father's Day without my dad. At any rate, my husband loved the card.

We were in New York, and I had a client who was in medical school there. She was at her family's house in Southern California for the summer, and she said we could stay in her apartment while she was gone. So that's what we did. Everything was on the tightest budget because adoption is expensive, and so is living in Southern California. When we got home from our trip, I was working one day, and Josh texted me, saying, *"Call me, call me."* When I did, he said that the attorney had called and said that we had been matched.

It's interesting how adoption works. There's an entire process, as you can imagine, but you sit down and essentially fill out a form of what characteristics you're willing to accept in your adopted child—and I mean everything, including the gender, ethnicity, and religion of the biological parents. I mean, there are so many different boxes that you can check.

They told us in the first meeting that the more checks you have, the longer the process will take. We'd heard that the adoption process could take a very long time for some people, but I wanted it to be quick. I also truly did not have any preferences. I trusted my faith to the point where I was like, whatever is going to be brought to us, it's going to be brought to us. So, I remember just drawing lines down the no-preference list on every single page.

Another part of the adoption process is writing a "Dear Birth Mother" letter. In this letter, you introduce yourself to the birth mother, sharing why she should choose you and what kind of life her child would have with you.

I believe that this process is designed this way for a reason, as are the adoption classes and the things they have you discuss. By the time we were done with our home study, I felt very equipped and emotionally ready to be a mother. I felt ready after all those classes, and we were also now CPR-certified. There were so many things that we had to do, but it was really cool for us to feel like we were progressing in parenthood before we even had a match.

So, now we had a match, and I didn't even ask him if it was a boy or a girl. I honestly didn't care. I was thrilled that we'd gotten a match within just a few months of starting the process. We set a date to meet the biological parents, and this was a rare situation because it was actually an expectant couple, whereas, typically, you're only meeting an expectant mother. If you've ever seen the movie *Juno*, Jennifer Garner plays this type of very overprepared, polished character. I sort of felt like I was her in that movie.

There was nothing that I was going to do to mess this entire date up. We met at Coco's in Brea, California. Coco's was a special restaurant to me. I didn't pick it, but I used to go there at least once a week with my "papa," probably my closest grandparent, who had passed away when I was twenty-three. It was kind of cool that we were now going to be meeting the potential birth parents of our child and our potential baby in someone's belly at such a restaurant that had such a special meaning to me.

We walked into Coco's, and our attorney was there at a table. As we sat down, I was so nervous. I remember going to the bathroom and having this little pep talk with myself, kind of trying to talk myself out of those feelings of inadequacy because they can play with your head while you're filling these books out, writing these birth mother letters, and essentially putting yourself in a catalog; you're selling yourself. I'm pretty sure I emailed our attorney on a weekly basis: *"People are seeing our book and not choosing us? Is there something I should change? I'll change anything."*

I was willing to change anything about myself so that I would be chosen. That comes from deep-rooted feelings of inadequacy and thinking that I'm not good enough. In my mind, I'd proven that my body wasn't good enough for motherhood, so why would I be good enough, then, for someone to choose me to be the mother of their child? We included pictures of our puppy in the book, and I remember thinking, *What if someone's a cat person? I don't want them not to choose us because we have a dog.* When I mentioned that to our attorney, he said, "You need to be patient. Someone will choose you for you. Your book is good because it is so much you two."

So, I had a little pep talk with myself in the bathroom, staring at myself in the mirror, telling myself, "Don't mess this up. Just be cool, be calm." I walked out, and there they were—and I was at a loss for what to say.

Going into this meeting, I would have said anything, but now I was speechless. I remember our attorney telling us, "We will know if it's a match almost immediately at dinner because of the way the conversation flows. We can just tell. It's like being on a first date. When there's chemistry between you, you can just tell."

I was so nervous that I started overthinking everything, which is totally normal. I did the same thing when I was actually dating, so this was not a surprise. We ended up having a great conversation and exchanging phone numbers at the end of it. I just fell in love with this couple, and it was unlike anything I'd ever experienced.

They didn't tell us anything right away. They had told us that there was one other couple that they had in mind first, which messed with my head a little bit, that I was their second choice. What could we have done better? Josh was like, "Just be grateful. They're going with us. We have their phone number, and we're going to be texting. This is awesome."

Then came the tango of, *Should I text or not? Am I texting too much? What if I send two texts in a row?* I was overthinking, overcompensating for my anxiety and feelings of inadequacy. I kept wondering, *What if she changes her mind and regrets choosing us?*

So, we messaged back and forth for the next few weeks. Our attorney had told us, "Be careful not to over-promise because when you want something, like a child, it's easy to want to promise the world to a potential birth mother. You don't need to do that. If it's a match, it's a match, so don't go down the road of making promises that you might not be able to keep."

We made a couple of appointments together, and I was really thinking, *This is awesome. Josh and I are going to see our baby's ultrasound*. Our expectant mother was about thirty weeks into the pregnancy, and we were going to get to see the baby.

We planned to get together with our family on the Fourth of July, and they texted us on the third to let us know that they were choosing us to be the parents. So, Josh and I were now officially expecting a baby girl, due in September of that year. It would be the perfect way to end a year that had started very traumatically. So, when we had our family over the next day for the holiday, we did a gender reveal with Silly String. This was our first celebratory event as expecting parents of a baby girl. There was so much joy on this day that feelings of inadequacy couldn't even chime in, because I was overfilled with hope for the future and thrilled that we were finally going to be past this hard chapter.

It's sort of crazy because it brought me back to the inadequacy that I felt when I was in my childhood, like I didn't really fit in. I had really strict parents, so from my perspective, it was as though I was a little inadequate compared to my friends. They'd say, "Oh, she's got strict parents. They're not going to let her go."

As I shared previously, I was labeled rebellious, so I was pretty much always in trouble. One time, they removed my bedroom door. I don't know if my dad just went to some parenting seminar at a very legalistic church, and they told him to do that, but losing my privacy and having no door to my room in high school was very traumatizing. My room was really the only place I could be fully me, as silly and goofy or as emotional as I wanted to be. It was my safe place.

Being more strict parents, they got me a cell phone as soon as I turned fifteen to keep a connection to me. From that point on, when I was in trouble, I'd be on restriction, and my phone would be taken away. Which I understand is typical, but I realize now that the trauma that it caused me was the withdrawal of the validation I got from communication with my friends. All feelings of acceptance went away when the phone did, because I didn't feel like I belonged in my home. I knew I was "loved and cared for," but accepted? That just wasn't what I felt.

One night, I was out and really wanted to have a good time with my friends. I probably just came off a week-long restriction. The boy I liked was going to be at a friend's house, so we all went there to hang out. I think we've all been in that scenario where you're at the same place as the guy you like, but you aren't sure if he likes you too. Come to find out, he did. So, I just completely forgot that my parents were supposed to be picking me up by a certain time. My cell phone, which was an old brick Nokia cell phone, had this snake-ringing sound, and I didn't realize that I had set it to the lowest volume possible.

Amidst my night of chatting with him, laughing, and just loving life, I walked by the table where I had left my purse. Back then (1999), people had phones but weren't attached to them like they are now. I checked my phone, and I saw that I'd had around forty missed calls—all from my parents! Freaking great! I was just having a good time, and now I am going to be in trouble. They ended up calling one of my friend's parents, who had the address of where we were. A few minutes later, my dad came barging through the door. It was like when a SWAT team breaks in. I remember my dad hunting in each room, looking for me, fueled with frustration because, to their knowledge, I had been purposefully ignoring them for hours. He finally found me, grabbed me by the arm, and marched me outside. This was by far the angriest I ever saw him.

I tried to apologize right away, "I'm sorry! I was just hanging out! Why are you so mad? It wasn't on purpose; no one else's parents are mad." But if I were a better communicator back then, I would have said, "I really wasn't intentionally avoiding you. I got carried away playing games, and my phone was silent on the counter. I am so sorry. We were all being safe, and I actually found out that the boy I liked also liked me, and we were having a great conversation. I did not ignore you on purpose. I am so sorry you were worried."

He chucked me in the car and said, "You're losing your phone, and you're losing your door." I was in so much trouble. I remember feeling like I had finally gotten this moment of acceptance, and now I was losing so much more than that. I just did not know how to communicate to my parents what I was feeling. I had already been labeled rebellious, and this was in alignment with the way a rebellious kid would act. I just felt completely inadequate and like I had no control. I just wanted to shut down and didn't even want to try anymore.

It was a very, very difficult time in my life. Going through adoption triggered many of those same emotions, feeling like I was waiting and that I had no control. I finally felt like I might be in a place where I was accepted in the same way as an expecting parent, but I wasn't, because I was not physically expecting. The same hard emotions reared their heads.

Every single person deals with this in some way, shape, or form. It mostly manifests as comparison. I talk to women every single day, and the one struggle every single woman seems to grapple with is comparison. I don't know a single person who doesn't compare themselves or their lives to others' in one way, shape, or form. This is rampant on social media, and it's designed to be that way: You get on, see what's happening with other people, and say to yourself, *I have a better situation than that, or I have a worse situation than that.*

Neither is really good because one can fuel your ego while the other can fuel feelings of inadequacy and just straight up rob you of your joy.

*** ACTION STEP ***

I encourage you to choose the area in which you feel inadequate. I want you to see yourself in the future or on the other side of whatever it is that makes you feel that way. Maybe you're just incapable at this point of really communicating it, but it's critical to identify what it is that you feel inadequate about and visualize yourself on the other side of it. What would it feel like? What would you do differently? I am a big believer that hope is motion-activated. What does that mean? Think about it like this: When you're using the restroom at a restaurant, and you go to wash your hands at an automated faucet, you don't just simply hope for the water to turn on; you have to put your hands under it to trigger the sensor. Hope is not waiting and wishing—it means you are taking action.

There's so much power in writing things down, telling ourselves positive affirmations, and talking things through because our brains often don't know what's real and what's fake. They only know the stories we tell ourselves. For example, I realized that when I was feeling inadequate, there was so much power in the way I spoke to myself. I would tell myself, *I'm not going to be able to do that,* and feelings of inadequacy would take over.

You may have very natural reasons to think that you are inadequate or less than, or perhaps, unbeknownst to you, you have been trained to think this way. The truth is that you just have a different path, different strengths, different talents, and a different story than everybody else.

So, the action step I'd like for you to take is to write down a list of your top five strengths. To do this most effectively, I recommend using the StrengthsFinders 2.0 assessment book by Gallup and Tom Rath. It helped me identify what my strengths were and how I could apply them, even in areas that seemed unrelated, like infertility, adoption, being a troubled teen, and even being forgetful. There are so many different ways that you can view perceived negatives as strengths.

Finding hope starts with seeing yourself in a positive light and speaking to yourself kindly. Words have incredible power—if you wouldn't say something to a friend, you're not allowed to say it to yourself. Okay? If you have someone in your life who can see the potential and beauty in you, you're a lucky person. Not everybody has that. So, my encouragement to you is to take the action step of writing down your top five strengths and identifying the situations in your life where they are the most activated. Identify the people who bring out the best in you and ask them what they believe are your top five strengths. For me, my feelings of inadequacy stemmed from my own insecurities. I often assumed people saw me a certain way, but when I changed my perspective, everything changed as a result.

I loved microphones from a very young age, me with one of my longest friends, Amie.

I love this picture of me with my mom.

This one makes me tear up every time I see it; my dad washing my hair as a baby. He was the best and I owe my career in hair to him.

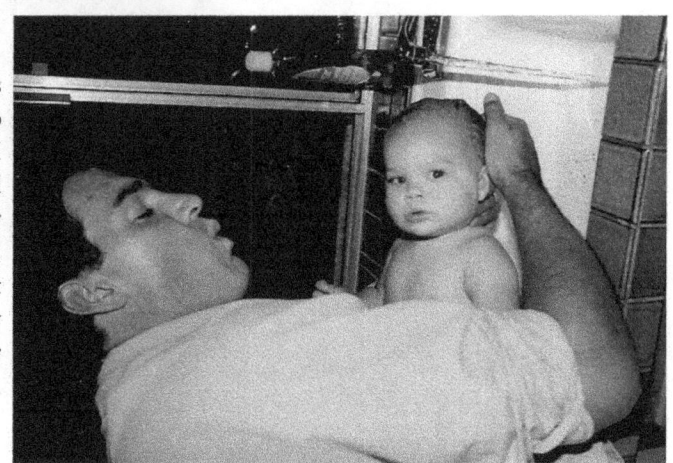

One of my favorite family photos.

This is one of my favorite photos and I pray Finley cherishes it also. She's with her two mothers who both love her so much.

The first time I got to hold Finley. She was about a week old and I had no idea this would be the day, it was a whirlwind of surreal emotions. She was so tiny.

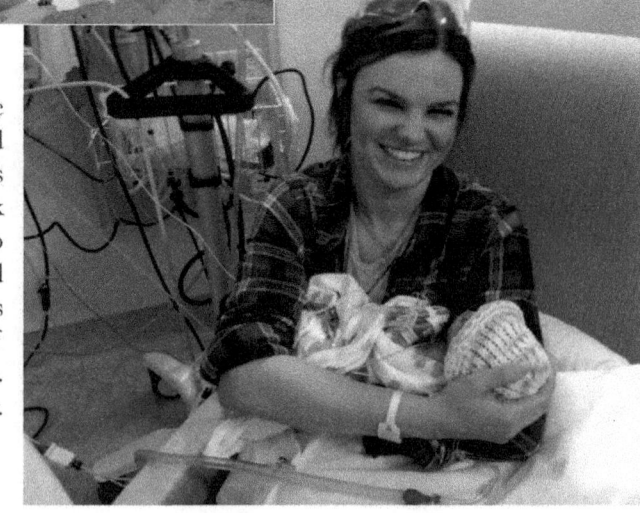

I wanted you to have a visual of the "life of the party Christina." Not to be confused with Christina Aguilera, hahahah. Just me and one of my best girlfriend's casually out front with a decorated house party sign. We later were each other's maids of honor.

My dad and I on my wedding day right before the ceremony. We laughed and cried the whole way until he handed me off to my groom. I miss him so much.

Working for Tamra has been one of the highlights of my career, I thank her often for the opportunity. I loved every second of it.

My handsome husband and I were married at Diver's Cove in Laguna Beach, California on June 17, 2011.

My beautiful family that I had to bribe for family photos, hahahah.

San Clemente Beach where their mom and dad fell in love and where we have grown into a family.

CHAPTER Five

PEOPLE PLEASING

In my past experience, the women I typically related to most were the ones I would gossip with. I have always viewed myself as a girl's girl and worked in salons with a female-only clientele. They don't call hairstylists "hairapists" for no reason. I loved my conversations, and I had the best clientele ever. I took it to the next level often—especially if I was hurt by someone—to gossip or be petty. These are not things I'm proud of, but I will one hundred percent acknowledge my behavior. I didn't realize how prevalent gossip was in my life until I had a few different situations happen where my mouth got me in trouble with the people I really wanted to please. I knew that I had a pattern of saying "yes" to people and not telling them how I really felt about things. This falls into standard people-pleasing struggles. You think you're doing everybody a favor by just agreeing and complying, but it really helps no one. Actually, you can easily end up being the bad guy in a situation.

So, it's not a healthy behavior at all, even though it feels like it might be because your ultimate goal is peace.

I started to become aware that I was maybe struggling with my female relationships in 2019. I found that I was having regular annual fallouts with different friends, in which I struggled with boundaries and speaking up. I would let things build up, and then, instead of dealing with them or telling the other person how I felt, I would just cut off the relationship or pick a fight about something else.

I'd cut them off for a year, and then we'd have some sort of text exchange, and there'd be a little bit of makeup. Then, a couple of years later, the cycle would repeat. So, I was constantly having drama with friends, and I totally thought that this behavior was normal in conjunction with everything else that I was going through on my different grief paths.

It all came to a head one night during a big blowout argument with my mom. She said, "Can't you see that you struggle with women?" I remember no other details, just this statement that struck me to the core and has stayed with me. I just know I tried to blame her for being the bad guy.

Truth is, I didn't want to see it; I couldn't handle that the common denominator of all my problems was me. I wanted to please everyone, except my mom. I didn't feel the need to be with her, so she kind of got this burnt end of me. Ultimately though, this is what sent me to therapy.

I had gotten into a different type of business besides hairstyling, one that involved building relationships with women and growing businesses together, and I absolutely loved it. I found so much reward in that versus simply providing someone with a beautiful cut and color for a few weeks. I found that this was a different way to develop myself because I was unhealed in so many ways. I'm very grateful that I began a journey of self-development and self-awareness through it. When you work solely with women and are forced to have these working relationships—you cannot avoid them, you cannot run away from them, you cannot numb yourself, and you have to face these things—being a people pleaser will be one of the first things about you that is exposed because there's no hiding or manipulating the truth.

I was once in a triangle of a situation with one of my mentors and one of my team members, and I was not helping the situation by inadvertently creating a wedge between them. I would tell one what I thought she wanted to hear, and I would tell the other one what I thought she wanted to hear. Finally, they had a conversation and found that I was making it worse. They realized that their main issues with each other had to do with what I'd said, so the lack of "peace" I was concerned about was because of me. That's what happens when you're not honest with people, and you choose "peace." The saying goes, you can sweep (you know what) under the rug, but it still stinks.

One of these ladies texted me and said, "Let's get on FaceTime." I did and was surprised to find that they were both on. It was one of the most difficult conversations I've ever faced, mostly because I was such an unhealed version of myself, but there was nowhere to run or hide, and there was no way that I could please both of these people at the same time. They called me out, "Christina said this," and "Christina said that," and it was all true, but my intentions were not what they appeared to be. I completely shut down. I cried. I had no words. I just felt the walls caving in.

When you struggle with people pleasing, your intentions are often misunderstood because your greatest motive is to make people not be mad at you. Due to the nature of my childhood and how I felt as though my parents and my teachers were always mad at me, I had created this safe bubble around myself. This made my clients love and adore me because I gave them really amazing hair, listened to their life stories, and was a safe space for them. Now, I was building this business where I was really able to help people, but a different type of relationship was involved; it was leadership now, which would no doubt expose my strengths *and* weaknesses.

The whole point of being successful is facing those things, identifying them, and having the awareness that the struggle is real, *but you can change it*. I did not realize that I could change it because I still had such a limited belief about what was possible for me. So, when I got off the Zoom call with the two ladies, I sobbed.

I had to face these people every day. I had to work with them. We had mutual relationships with hundreds of people, and many are very public. It can seem so trivial from the outside, but when you're in that situation, honestly, it seems like nothing else exists. I've been through a lot of hard stuff, and let me tell you, this was one of the hardest because it involved so many people, and there was no controlling the narrative. And you know how it is at work when things spread; it can make or break your reputation.

When I woke up the next day, the first thing I thought was, *Oh, my gosh, did that really happen? Do they really hate me now? What am I going to do?* To my surprise, one of them, who lived really close to me, brought me coffee and hugged me.

I just remember thinking, *You should be really mad at me, and here you are, giving me grace.* This was not something I was used to. Usually, when I got in trouble, my nose got mushed in it like I was a bad puppy. So, with this, I was really taken by the grace that I was given. Being quick to forgive is powerful for so many reasons, but I was still very hard on myself about the whole situation. As I shared in a previous chapter, I had been surprised by a three-way call, just as my girlfriend had set me up years before to trick me into confessing to cheating on my boyfriend. This triggered *many* old emotions in me.

I just shut down. I remember thinking, *Okay, I need therapy because I need to be able to tell people what I'm thinking. I feel like I'm a doormat, and why am I allowing myself to be treated this way?*

I had such a unique perspective on the whole mess of a situation I had created for myself. I saw myself as the victim somehow, even though I was not the victim; that's how I saw it. I thought, *I'm going to therapy because I want to fix everybody else.* I remember asking a few of my clients, who were very open about going to therapy, who they recommended. Once I settled on one, I made an appointment and began setting up my visits with her. My whole point in going was to change the way that I saw everybody else, but it ended up having a different result after months and months and months of visits with her.

It honestly reminds me of the first time that I got drunk with my friends. I was in junior high, and our little group of girlfriends was really tight, but we would kind of rotate who was going to be on the outs. I had the "strict" parents, I was the one singing show tunes when everyone else was singing "Blink-182," and I didn't have the coolest clothes or other things. When it was my turn to be on the outs, it was so painful for me because of everything that I was experiencing and all those emotions I felt. I'd think, *All I want is for these people to like me, and they don't like me right now. What can I do to make them like me?* I found myself changing who I was in a lot of ways so that people would maybe like me.

The first time I got drunk was at my girlfriend's house, which most people would call a mansion. It was the kind of house that had a library and a dining room with its own set of doors.

It was a slumber party with about six of us, and we got into her dad's triple sec, an orange liqueur. I have no idea why we chose that—probably because it was the least touched—but that's what we went with.

Sleepovers put a lot of extra pressure on me because I always worried that the other girls would want to go "TP" houses. My parents had given me very specific instructions that I was not allowed to do that, and they'd said that I would be in grave trouble if I did. So, I remember thinking, *Please, dear God, do not let them say that they want to go toilet papering because it's either going to force me to really be uncool and say I'm not going, or to get in major trouble because all my friends are doing it, and I am the queen of doing what my friends are doing.* Alcohol seemed like a better alternative to me because we wouldn't be leaving the house. I just laughed out loud writing that; this was really how I thought.

As we drank, I went from being the girl who was just trying to fit in with the group to leading the charge of the fun, the games, and making everybody laugh. I don't know how drunk I was, but I loved the feeling of everybody enjoying me and my strengths.

For so long, I told that story and never really realized its true power until I sat down and identified all the hard emotions that I went through and the hopeless times that I faced. I could really see the connection between the past and the present, and I've continued to deal with the same things that I've dealt with since junior high.

Your power comes from you. It is not dependent on whether or not people like you. As a matter of fact, the times that I am the unhappiest with myself to this day are the times when I do something with the intention of impressing someone or getting in someone's good graces. I still struggle with pleasing people in some way, shape, or form, but now I've gotten to a place where, instead of living to please others, I live to please my family and do what's best for us as a unit, with integrity as the baseline standard.

A lot of times, that means saying no without apology, saying no without feeling like I need to explain myself. I learned that I'm not just going to give someone else the power to dictate my emotions for the day. But I still slightly struggle with it; I'll always combat that initial instinct to please. I trust my secondary thought, which is more prominent: to have a very good boundary. In the beginning, it was hard to set boundaries, and I got upset if people tried to push them. And now I will actually get more mad at *myself* if I break a boundary I set. It really is an incredibly freeing feeling when you are on the other side of being a people-pleaser.

There are things you can do to help identify exactly where and what your boundaries should be, and how you can help yourself get out of such situations. No one is going to be able to turn off other people's opinions of you. They're always going to be there. You're always going to let someone down. But if you are enough for yourself, you're not letting yourself down, and you can create clear boundaries and communicate them to others; there's so much freedom in that. And it's so much closer than you think. I remember thinking that I'd be talking about myself like this when I was eighty years old. That maybe, one day, I would be free of caring what people think. But I'm not even forty, and I have finally figured this out. I want everyone to understand it, too; it's one of the reasons I devoted an entire chapter to the subject and speak about it quite frequently on my podcast and social media.

It's so imperative to realize that you are much closer to having this freedom than you think. I recommend therapy and facing whatever it is because the sooner you do, the sooner you can get through it. That's just how it works. Right now, we can let these little molehills become mountains in our brains because that's what we're telling ourselves they are. When you face it, you can silence it. It's an unbelievable thing. You can move and grow past pleasing people, and it will free your life.

*** ACTION STEP ***

Here's my action step for you regarding this. The next time that you find yourself apologizing for saying no, I want you to take it back. Every time I start to type out, "I'm sorry," I delete it. Instead, I'm like, *Nope. I don't need to apologize for that. This is my boundary.*

It's different, obviously, if you've let someone down or truly wronged them, but a lot of times, it starts with unnecessarily apologizing for just having a thought, having an opinion, or being who you are. I've had to learn the difference between what warrants an apology and what doesn't. So, take it back and stop apologizing for yourself. Identifying that habit is key to rewiring your brain so that you no longer apologize for being yourself.

I also want you to practice saying no. Instead of instinctively saying yes because you think it will please the people around you, ask yourself, *What do I really want? What am I doing that I really don't want to be doing and shouldn't have to be doing and am even apologizing for not doing?* Identify it and write it down, and the next time you start to apologize, stop yourself.

CHAPTER Six

NUMBING

I knew that alcohol was not making me a better version of myself. Does it really make anyone better? If there were a scorecard, I would venture to guess that alcohol would rate lowest on what improves a human's experience with you. I had struggled with moderating my intake. I had definitely overdone it on multiple occasions and had to make my rounds of apologies. I had increased anxiety around it, and I had never been pregnant, so I never really had to go any amount of time without drinking.

A couple of times, I told myself that I was going to take a break, give it up for Lent, or hit the pause button on it, but with my feelings of inadequacy and people-pleasing and after the grief that I had been through, I lived with this YOLO (you only live once) mentality, and every single thing became a celebration. Now that you know a little bit more about my history, you can see why I wanted to always be the girl who was celebrating, because it was the quickest way to avoid anybody feeling sorry for me and to get people to want to hang out with me. If I'm always having fun, being funny, and being the life of the party, then hello! Mission accomplished: acceptance.

So, that's essentially where my drinking stemmed from. But if you go one layer deeper, there's also my resentment of my mom and myself for not growing a backbone sooner. This deeper issue was born early in my life from many things. I was actually diagnosed with rosacea in my early thirties, and I didn't believe anybody who said, "We should get to the root of the problem." I thought, *Nope, if there's a medication for that, I'm going to take it.* It's such a metaphor for my life because I was all about these band-aids and not actually getting to the root of any problem. Short-term comfort typically means long-term discomfort is underway.

I had tried to get sober a couple of times, but it didn't work because there was always something to celebrate. In any three-week span, if you think that there's nothing to celebrate, you're wrong. There's a holiday, there's the weekend, there's a Tuesday... there was always something. So, it just wasn't going to be possible for me.

I was on a kick of clearing my skin and trying a more holistic approach. I had a friend on my team who had healed her acne and was into all these natural detoxes. I reached out to her to help me, and she had me do this thing called a stool test. I was into it; it was exciting to me. So, we did the test, and the first results were that my body was not absorbing any nutrients.

I thought to myself, *That's kind of weird.*

And she said, "Yeah, I thought for sure you would have candida overgrowth." That was such a hot topic at the time, and everybody was talking about candida overgrowth. She said, "How much wine do you drink?"

I replied, "What do you mean? Could that really be causing a problem?"

"If you have too much alcohol in your body," she replied, "it will inhibit your body from absorbing nutrients."

That genuinely made me think, *Wow, okay, so this is not good.* "I can definitely cut back," I said, "and I can do a detox."

This went on for quite a few more months, and I attempted to cut back on my drinking. She prescribed me all these supplements, and I got off medication. I had a perpetual antibiotic drug that I would use anytime I wanted my skin clear before an event or a trip, which was often, as my business began to take off; I was always going somewhere. Which meant I was "on" and drinking. I was able to get off medication cold turkey! Alcohol is another story.

One day in February 2020, I went to church with my husband. At that point, my drinking hadn't been a topic for a few months. It was just a regular Sunday. I walked into church happily after dropping Finley off with her "sidekick"—the church had a program for special needs parents that assigned their children a one-on-one caretaker called a sidekick.

As I was singing worship, *BAM!*—a feeling came over me, and I suddenly knew I needed to stop drinking. The thought just shot into my brain. I turned to my husband, grabbed his arm, and said, "I need to give up alcohol and never drink again. I feel like God just told me not to drink."

I kept singing but was pretty weirded out—it was **not** from my brain. When the song ended, I looked at Josh and said, "Seriously, don't let me drink."

This was not the first time I had asked him to do that, but it had been a few years, so he nodded assuredly at me and replied, "Okay."

I just said, "I'm not supposed to drink anymore." And I really believed that I would never drink again. As a matter of fact, to this day, I have not had a drink since February 2020.

A crazy thing happened along with this—and I say "crazy" because I believe that it's crazy how you can be completely tested the moment you decide that you're going to do something really good for yourself. You will be faced with things that make it really hard for you to keep that promise.

Finley turned five, and we really wanted to adopt again. Josh felt it in his heart that we should go the foster adoption route, so we did. He rarely has a super strong opinion on these big decisions we've made over the years, so I was completely okay with giving him this one. Within days of posting on social media that we were hoping to adopt again, I had a family friend DM me asking if we were open to twins (more on that beautiful story later).

The twins had come to live with us when they were eighteen months old, and, at that time, wine was a nightly enjoyment for me. I had just created that routine for myself. I'd fallen completely into mommy wine culture. I mean, I had t-shirts that said *"Wine Time"* on them. I had legit gear for wine! I didn't love feeling a little sluggish after bath and bedtime, but I had just kept telling myself it was normal and that all moms feel like this. And honestly, it kept all of my hard emotions at bay. There was nothing aside from this random day at church and the words from God that was going to actually be the thing that stopped me.

So here's the **crazy** story of how it got more difficult to give up alcohol. I'm aware it's odd, but it's true (lol).

Now that the twins were living with us, I was getting used to having three car seats in the first row of my tall Escalade. My daughter Finley was diagnosed with cerebral palsy due to her premature birth, so she required help with everything. Getting three kids up and loaded into the car was a task in itself. To make my life easier, I removed the armrest on her booster seat from the side where I loaded her into the car so I could just back in easily—if that makes sense.

One day, I was putting one of the twins, Samantha, in the car when I hopped into the backseat and onto Finley's booster seat—seems normal, right? However, since I had removed the armrest, a sharp, rectangular piece of plastic was exposed. Think of a large cookie cutter.

Well, I landed squarely on that piece of plastic with all my weight—plus Samantha's—right in the center of my crotch. I had **jumped** with full force and come down hard on it. The result? The worst hematoma you could ever imagine. It looked like I was growing male genitalia. It was unbelievable, but no one believed me. I couldn't exactly post pictures, but my friends who saw it in person cringed and covered their mouths. I could barely walk, and sitting was just as painful.

I had spoken with so many women who had had hematomas from birth, who said that a hematoma in that area was more painful than their childbirth experience. Anytime I bent to help Finley, I'd feel the most pinching, painful experience I'd ever had. I so wanted to drink because of how uncomfortable it was. I went to the doctor because I wanted someone to check it out since it looked bad. The swelling was horrific, and the pain was so gnarly that I knew I needed medical care.

They sent me to get an ultrasound right away. On my way to get it, a hundred million thoughts were in my head: *How could such a fluke accident like this have happened? How am I this accident-prone?* Also, when you're going through the foster process, you can't just leave your kids with anyone; they must also be foster-certified if it's going to be over a certain amount of time. It was the most chaotic thing. I feel like that's how so many people's lives are: The moment they try to really take charge, that's when all hell breaks loose.

When I got the ultrasound, the guy doing it didn't really believe me when I told him how it happened. I mean, I guess it is kind of hard to believe that such a tiny little square could cause such a huge issue.

But am I the type of responsible adult who takes care of these things? No. I was scared, so I made an appointment, but I did keep on with my normal routine. I went to a coffee date with a few girls on my team and was kind of laughing about how random the injury was when I got a call from Kaiser.

The doctor was very concerned about where it was on my body and explained that it was really close to the part of the groin where a main artery goes straight to the heart. They were worried that if any tiny piece of this major hematoma sent a blood clot into that artery, it could be fatal. And I just remember being like, *I just got these children, and I just decided to give up alcohol. I want to drink more than anything at this point in my life. Like, what in God's name is happening right now?*

For the entire hour-long drive to the doctor's office, I sat on a donut and leaned to the left. I just remember praying, "If I can have this just be nothing and have it go away, I will live my life in such a way that I will do my best with what I've got and bring people to peace and healing, sharing all my stories, even the ones that are embarrassing, and I will do my best to help as many people as possible. I will give you all of me, God, and give up alcohol." I called Josh on the way, telling him what they had said about how serious it was. It was strange: This very funny thing that had happened was now very dangerous.

I got to the doctor's office, and they did another scan. Then I was told, "I don't know why they worried you so much. You're going to be fine. This thing looks fine." Despite the whiplash I felt, that made me smile. I mean, not even an ounce of me wanted to be mad that they'd gotten me worried. I believe in miracles, so I was totally open to the fact that maybe this was due to the promise that I had made. I don't think I've ever been so happy to be in so much pain.

At home, I had a bottle of wine that I kept for whatever reason. I just had it there. It kind of felt like a security blanket. At this point, I hadn't had a drink for about two weeks. When I got home from the doctor's office, one of the first things I did was dump it out. I felt like I was actually taking charge. I was filled with gratitude and so full of life, even with the unbearable pain! As I reflected on different emotions and laughed at myself, I thought, *How was this my actual life? Who does this?*

The question I asked myself in my head—*Why can't you be more careful, Christina?*—transported me back to when I was about nine years old, just after being scolded for being accident-prone. I could see that little girl, who meant no harm, feeling embarrassed and ashamed after breaking the glass mirror. I zoned deeply into that memory, remembering how huge those emotions felt.

All of a sudden, the blurred noise of my dissociation snapped me back into reality. Here I was, a grown adult, facing this silly little accident—one that ended up being a key moment in changing my life and rewriting the story I had so often told myself about *"accident-prone Christina."*

My mom's name is Gina, and my kids call her Gigi, so I'm going to use that for the remainder of the book. I've shared a lot about how I grew up and that my relationship with my mom was less than ideal. Of course, *now* we are great and have a very mature relationship. I was so honored that she agreed to write the foreword to this book. If you are going through a hardship with your mom or daughter, here's a little sprinkle of hope thrown at you! **There is hope.**

Gigi had her own childhood traumas that wired her a certain way, and, of course, as a result, they wired me a certain way too. I know my kids will sit in therapy one day because of the way I'm influencing their wiring.

I grew up in such a neat and orderly home that you could see vacuum lines on the carpet in our front living room almost all the time. My mom would know if I had walked into that room because the carpet would have footprints on it. It was basically an off-limits room. The rest of the house was tidy, with its fair share of little knick-knacks and picture frames—but everything had its place.

Honestly, it felt a little like growing up in a museum—look but don't touch. If you've seen my home, you now understand exactly where that wiring came from. My house could not be emptier, and I blame my childhood. I'm laughing as I write this, but all jokes aside, the minimalist apple didn't fall far from the asylum tree. Everything was dusted regularly. Since Gigi was a stay-at-home mom, our house was always in order. She wasn't quite at Howie Mandel's level of OCD, but I often called her a "clean freak."

And then there was me, this little dirty bull in the china closet. Growing up, I smashed every single one of my fingers on different occasions. Sometimes, they needed medical attention; sometimes, it was just a smashed fingernail. Turns out, they grow back. I was so careless about my physical appendages that they got smashed in trunks, doors, windows, and everything.

When I was in the second grade, one of the wildest accidents of my life happened. I grew up with only a couple of girls on my street; most of my neighbors were boys. And I, obviously, was boy crazy. Remember, I was on a quest for love that started in kindergarten, so I absolutely loved being surrounded by and trying to keep up with the boys. It was a regular day after school. Everyone was out rollerblading, and a few of the boys were visiting their dad's house for the weekend. Rollerblades were all the rage, and I couldn't miss out on the action.

Next to our house was a steep driveway, and at the very top of our cul-de-sac, there was a random little concrete hill with a sewer lid on top—it was almost straight down. The boys had created an unofficial figure-eight track, zooming from one hill to the next on their blades.

I went up a few times but chickened out. Still, something in me said, *Do you have it?!* **guts?!** There was an after-school show on

Nickelodeon called "GUTS," and I did, in fact, have them. So I thought, *Okay, I'm going to do it too.*

Well, somehow, I did it successfully a couple of times. I felt really cool and was getting the hang of it. I was so thrilled to be doing what the cool boys were doing that I didn't notice that on my third go-round, there was a newspaper on the driveway we were going down. I tripped over it, and the only thing I knew to do was to put my arms out to break my fall. I felt a crack in both of them as I was going really fast on rollerblades down a hill. I immediately thought, *I am in pain; this is not good,* and I started screaming.

One of my dad's jobs at the time was giving pitching lessons in our backyard, which meant there were always really cute boys around while I was growing up. Imagine if Southern California's best baseball pitchers—of all ages—had a central hub. That hub was my house.

A few went on to be pretty famous, too. When he heard me screaming, he cleared the five-foot cinderblock wall from our backyard and came flying into the front yard. I rolled onto my back, screaming and crying, and he said, "Move your hands like this." He gestured for me to flex my wrists back and forth. I was able to do it, but it really, really, really hurt. "Okay, you're fine," he said. "They're not broken," and he went about his day.

That was enough blading for one day. I was pretty embarrassed, so I went inside (I left my dirty clothes in the garage first, of course), took a bath, and rested. I didn't complain too much at dinner or bedtime, but something didn't feel right.

The next morning, when I woke up, my wrists were locked. I could not move them at all. My mom was like, "Oh, this isn't good," and she took me to the doctor. It turns out, as luck would have it, I had broken both of my wrists at the same time. The left arm had a slightly worse fracture, so I got a beautiful cast all the way up to my elbow on my left arm and a cast up to my forearm on the right. And there I was, this little second-grade bruiser with two broken arms. That is the classic depiction of my childhood and how accident-prone I was.

I remember telling everybody, "I told my parents that my arms were broken, and they didn't believe me." I finally felt like I'd had a moment where something I'd said was true, but no one believed me. I've told this story so many times over the years. It's kind of like one of those you tell when you're playing two truths and a lie or going around a circle and sharing a "fun fact"—you know, I broke both wrists at the same time. So, it's something that I talk about with ease, but I didn't realize the amount of resentment I carried toward my parents because of it. That resentment just kind of blew up later in my life, and it wasn't until therapy that I realized that I needed to deal with it.

Actually, resentment is very connected to rosacea. Now, that may seem weird, but it absolutely is. The different emotions that we harbor can make us sick in different ways. We're in a generational situation where we have all these different outlets to distract us and get us to feel comfortable, but they actually make it easy to avoid the things we need to deal with. For a lot of people, resentment is at the root of many different issues.

I remember thinking it was a little "woo-woo" that resentment would be linked to rosacea. At this point, I was not very in tune with my emotions or patterns, or into self-development at all. You, too, might think that it's sort of ridiculous that there would be a link between the two, but our emotions really do manifest in our bodies, just in unusual ways. There's actually a lot of information out there to back that up. You just have to be willing to look for it and have an awareness of it.

So, I sat in therapy, and I worked through every single ounce of trauma, everything I was resisting, everything I was avoiding, and the biggest underlying factor was the major resentment I was holding. I wasn't even aware that I had been feeling this much resentment in so many different ways.

It wasn't the way that you would think that it would look. It wasn't super hostile, and it wasn't super angry; it was just more sensitive, more reactive emotionally, and it was nothing that I thought a textbook version of resentment would be. What I would like to teach you with this is that when you are unable to forgive, it only hurts you. I think we've all heard the saying that being unwilling to forgive someone is like drinking poison and hoping that it hurts the other person. That is so true.

You may even be harboring negative emotions for someone you don't even realize that you need to forgive. One of the key indicators is how you feel around them. Can they set you off by saying one small thing? That might be an indicator that there's an underlying factor. But we all practice a set of patterns in different situations. If you find yourself experiencing the same emotions over and over and over, it's a key indicator that you need to change the habits that are perpetuating that cycle.

I love the movie *Yes Man*. It is one of my favorites. If you haven't seen it, I highly recommend that you do so. It's a Jim Carrey film, and it cracks me up. Tony Robbins is in it, too.

In essence, the main character is a guy who says no to everything, but he doesn't like the direction his life is headed. He goes to this conference, and the guru says, "Start saying yes to everything." So, the main character gets into the habit of saying yes, and it completely changes his entire life. In the end, he is like, "Who knew that just saying yes instead of saying no was going to evolve my life into this beautiful, fun adventure?"

I am living proof that you can truly change the direction of your life by having an awareness of your hard emotions that you don't want to deal with. You can disrupt a pattern by changing a habit, and it will completely change the direction of your life.

I had a falling out with my family for about a year in 2020. I know a lot of people can relate to that because it was such an unusual time, and there was so much division amongst families and friends and people in general. But I remember meeting up with one of my family members for coffee a year later, and it had been such a transformative time for me. I was actually going to AA. I was in therapy, too, and doing all this work. Part of the program had me go around and make amends with all the people I had unresolved issues with.

I really believe that this act of forgiveness and accountability was so powerful in terms of moving me forward in my life. When I put my head on my pillow at night, I know that I don't have any unresolved issues out there. I can't tell you how good that feels, and not everybody reciprocated or accepted the apology, and some didn't even respond to my messages. But as my dad would always say, "Keep your side of the street clean," and I really felt like my side of the street was the cleanest it had ever been, and that was the greatest weight off my shoulders.

So, if you feel like you're carrying anything, forgiveness is where it's at. And even though what you might be carrying is a very traumatic, unforgivable thing that you've experienced, there's something about releasing it and giving it out and not letting it have power over you that is so, so, so powerful. You don't have to hold on to that guilt or shame or anything that comes along with something that happened to you. Trust me, I completely understand, and I'll be sharing about that in the next chapter. But forgiveness is not reconciliation. After I met with my family member, they told me that it seemed like they were out to coffee with a completely different person than the one they had known their whole life.

My call to action for you in this chapter is inspired by something that had a profound impact on my life, thanks to Tony Robbins.

I attended one of his conferences and really connected with the energy—changing your body posture, getting into a peak state where your body feels its best. Your body language can reflect your emotions; for example, when your shoulders are hunched, it can signify feeling depressed or low-energy. Changing your posture can influence how you feel emotionally. Standing tall with your shoulders back can boost confidence and reduce stress, while slouching may reinforce feelings of sadness or fatigue. Your body sends signals to your brain, so how you hold yourself physically can help shift your mental state. He says to start by getting your body right before you can get your mind right. So when I'm feeling down and want to change that, I simply adjust my body language. Sit up taller, take a deep breath, and get ready for the next instructions.

*** ACTION STEP ***

A lot of people might be tempted to skip this action plan, but don't—you have to do it, okay? You bought this book, you've nodded along, and we've likely laughed and cried together through these chapters. Don't miss out on one of the most freeing exercises!

Okay, ready? I want you to write down a list of people you need to forgive—maybe even people who need to forgive you. Just because you don't feel the need to enter a program or don't have a heavy burden on your mind doesn't mean you won't benefit from this.

Every single person carries something unresolved with someone else. So, take a moment. Make a list of people you need to forgive or those who may need to forgive you. Then, take the step—either forgive them or ask for forgiveness.

It's fine to just practice writing a letter to this person or draft a text message. So many times, it helps me just to sit down and write the text message and then ponder or sit on it before sending. But if you can get together with that person, whether it's for coffee, having them over, or dropping something off for them, just try it and watch what happens in your life and the freedom that you're going to feel from it. You may have to face a hard conversation. You may have to face reconciliation. But right now, nothing's getting better with the harboring of these negative emotions, and there's no other way to move forward.

You bought this book for a reason, and you want your life to move forward for a reason. You're going to have to lean into the hard things to get through them. I know you're probably imagining at least one person right now that you are absolutely not going to reach out to or forgive. I want you to write a letter to them and start with, *"I forgive you."* Then, write out your feelings. Write out what you want to say and tell them how you're no longer letting it have power over you. I'm not saying to send it. I'm just saying to write it down, watch how your feelings start to flow, and be mindful of any kind of accountability that you can take in the situation. This will be hard.

Every time I share about my mom and our relationship, people come up to me and say, "I wish my mom could hear this," or "I wish my daughter could hear this," as though it's a one-way street when it comes to who needs to hear it. One of the things that my mom and I worked through in our relationship was that we both took accountability. That was the only way that we were able to move forward, heal our relationship, and go from fighting regularly and not speaking to not seeing each other for an entire year, to sharing a stage to tell our story. That's because both parties have taken extreme accountability and even almost want to claim fault for the whole thing instead of blaming each other. That comes with true forgiveness. So guess what? **You** are the one hearing this, which means the forgiveness ball is in your court.

CHAPTER *Seven*

GUILT & SHAME

Finley was about fifteen months old when she was officially diagnosed with cerebral palsy. Growing up, I had seen people using wheelchairs, walking with a limp, and using walkers, but I never knew what it meant. I had an awareness, but I did not actually know cerebral palsy existed. It was a whole new world for me to have a child with this disability, just learning the ins and outs of it.

We had an idea that she had CP because she was born nine weeks early and suffered grade 3 bilateral brain bleeds. Typically, any type of brain injury where there's a lack of oxygen, bleeding in the brain, or injury to the brain can result in a type of cerebral palsy. There are many types, which is why, when they first discovered the bleeding, they told us that she might not ever walk or talk. They also said, "She might be fine; only time will tell."

So, I went straight into looking at all the things I could do. There was no way I was going to sit around hopelessly. God made me capable and put this baby in our lives via adoption. I was **chosen** to be her mother, so I began my journey as a special needs mom and advocate. I quickly discovered there are alternative ways that you can rewire your brain and help create neural pathways when there might be an injury in part of the brain.

There are numerous therapies, early interventions, and procedures that can help with this. So many things exist now, but eleven years ago, the information was a little bit harder to find. Right now, you could do a quick Instagram search and find countless families and resources showcasing what life with cerebral palsy looks like (and I love that for this generation). But back then, there wasn't much on the internet at all. In truth, I only found a couple of stories—mostly sad, full of doom and gloom—which was definitely not my vibe.

Then I found one woman who was sharing her son Austin's story on Instagram. She would dress him up in cute mommy-and-me outfits, and she seemed to be thriving in her life while sharing the hardships. This gave me a visual of what I could expect for us.

The thing that stood out to me the most was that she had a smile on her face. I had so much guilt surrounding raising Finley —guilt that I was raising someone else's child, that someone had chosen me to be a parent, and that I was robbing her biological mother of the life that she could have had with her child. Even when Finley was in the hospital, I remember several of the NICU nurses, before we signed the adoption papers, sort of giving off that energy to me like I was taking this young woman's baby.

It's so interesting because you don't necessarily think about these different emotions and scenarios until you're *in* those shoes. Then it's like, *What am I supposed to do with this guilt?* Honestly, there's even a little bit of shame, which is weird because most people think of adoption as a beautiful thing, but there are hard emotions that come along with it. Receiving Finley's diagnosis was one of those bittersweet moments because it unlocked different resources and new doors for us. Once we had a diagnosis, then we could pursue different options.

We had several doctors who didn't even want to put it on her paperwork or her medical record because they didn't want the label to follow her. Looking back, I don't really understand that because she clearly had cerebral palsy. That wasn't going to be what was going to make her life difficult; the label was going to be what made her life simpler.

The first time that I had an interaction about her diagnosis, I had been sort of a recluse. Becoming a mother was a very difficult transition for me emotionally. I think it's because I went straight from my dad dying right into, two months later, the infertility diagnosis. Then, just a handful of months later, we were holding our 3.9-pound preemie who suffered a traumatic brain injury, and I was in an ICU again, hearing the all-triggering beeping and smelling the same smells as when I'd watched my dad die.

Now, I was in the same exact situation, just with my child, and hopefully, I was going to be watching her get better. I worried that she might die, and it was a whirlwind of a six-month period. Going straight from all of that into the adoption classes had made us feel very prepared, but with a child who was born so prematurely and who had so many medical needs, I became paranoid. I didn't let anyone touch her. I didn't let anyone feed her. I was a Velcro mom. I was very scared and felt so many things all the time.

This was also the first time that I wasn't able to work. Even when my dad was dying, and I received my infertility diagnosis, I went to work. In fact, I sort of became a workaholic. So, when all of that came to a screeching halt, and I was paranoid, obsessive, and on this quest for my baby, it really changed me. I know motherhood changes people. I think there's a set of expectations that you have about the beautiful ways it's going to change you, but not all the hard ways. With neurologist appointments, ophthalmologist appointments, special medical appointments, pain management doctors, neurosurgeon appointments, brain ultrasounds, hip X-rays, eye surgery, and being at weekly early intervention appointments, it was all a lot for my very unhealed version of myself.

I did the best that I could, but I withdrew from a lot. I could not deal with being around other people because of the guilt and shame that I didn't even realize I was carrying around with me. Part of me felt guilty that the vision I'd had of chasing my baby down the hall in her diaper had just evaporated, and I lost hope for what that was going to look like. How would I even say that to people? They would only say that she was healthy because, no matter what situation you're in, someone is always going to have it worse.

Thankfully, I did have a baby who was meeting her milestones; she was just meeting them later than typical children. She could suck her bottle by herself. She could sit up with a propped pillow. She could roll herself over to the right. She did have so many abilities, but at the same time, I had a fifteen-month-old who was barely just learning how to crawl, and I was navigating feeling proud and then also feeling guilty about it.

I never once wished my life were different. That might be

unusual, but I never wished for a different life. Instead, my attitude was, *Okay, this is happening. What am I going to do with it?* I never really questioned a lot of things. I think that stemmed from the attitude I had at a young age that hard things happened to me. I didn't even question it anymore. But I felt like I was a part of it. I truly felt guilty.

The one thing that sticks out to me the most is the first time I dealt with CP and the icky feelings that came with it. Remember, I'm the person who does not want anyone to pity me at all, and that definitely goes for my child as well. We were at therapy one day, and we were so fortunate to get a loaner gait trainer, which is a pull-around-the-body wheeled machine that you can sit your child in, and there's a seat with holes that they can put their legs through. So, they are sturdily in there, sort of suspended in like a bucket swing in the middle of these wheels. It allows them not to have to carry or bear all their weight, but they can still move their legs and propel themselves forward. They were very expensive, and there was a waitlist for them. Insurance takes forever.

So, we got this loaner, and I was grateful for how much those wheels changed my heart and my life in so many ways. Finley was practicing walking, and her therapy appointment was right next door. It was a medical center, so there were other offices there. A man walked by and said, "What's wrong with her?"

I looked at him, stunned, because, in my mind, this was my precious baby. I'd become such a recluse that nobody had said something like this to me before, let alone a stranger. Everyone who knew our situation was either my friend or was following our journey on Instagram. I was speechless. I had nothing to say. I just stared at him. And then the therapist spoke up and said, "Nothing's wrong with her. Her body just moves a little differently."

Afterward, I cried the entire way home. Number one, I was upset that I didn't know how to defend my child. Number two, I hadn't even seen it that way until the therapist said it. It really changed how I felt about the guilt I was carrying because I was now able to see things in such a beautiful way.

There was nothing wrong with my daughter. She just did things differently. Even today, that's the mentality I have. Nothing's wrong. It's just different from what you're used to seeing. I think a lot of that mentality comes from the way I feel life just happens to us, and then it's up to us to deal with it, although I do want to take accountability for anything I've set in motion.

When I was right out of high school, I was still very aimless. I loved socializing. I loved partying. I loved forgetting everything, and I also loved to shock people. I had learned that shock value was funny. I had learned that I could be alive at parties. I had learned all these different unhealthy coping mechanisms for life, ways to avoid, become numb, and escape. I went to a junior college, but some of my girlfriends went to a university, and I sort of party-hopped around town. On any day or night, I could walk into a bar, club, restaurant, or pub, and I knew everybody there. I took so much pride in that and getting to know everybody. I loved feeling important in that way. Networking. I mean, truly, that's what it was at the end of the day. It was just good old-fashioned networking, just with a side of drugs and alcohol.

One night, I was out with one of my girlfriends, and I had a really awful situation happen. I had told my parents that I would be staying with my friends at the university that they attended, and we were going to be hanging out with one of the girls, her guy friends, and some other people.

At this point in my life, I was notorious for having a bad attitude if I didn't want to be somewhere. My girlfriend used to have to literally ask me to be nice to people: "Christina, can you please be really nice to them?" I found that I was kind of rude to men. I had no idea where that came from. I don't know if it was just the heartbreak, but remember, I identified hardcore as a girl's girl.

That night, a guy was there whom I did not want anything to do with. I really didn't like this guy and didn't want him around me. Absolutely not. Yet I drank a lot of cheap vodka from my red Solo cup. Maybe it was "jungle juice." Whatever it was, I blacked out, and the next morning, I had several memories of being intimate with him. That was probably the most shameful I have ever felt. Number one, I couldn't remember a lot of it, which ended up being a big blessing, I guess.

But number two, I knew and was fully aware that something had happened. I needed to do something about it because I was not on any kind of birth control, and I didn't want to have a situation where I had to live with the memory of this for my entire life. I was nineteen and terrified.

I remember telling my girlfriend that I needed to go to Planned Parenthood. She mentioned hearing that there was a clinic on campus that offered Plan B. Because I wasn't a student there, I had to ask my very pure and responsible girlfriend to go get it for me. This was probably the grossest I've ever felt. I was very hungover, but the guilt was the most sickening, and the shame was overwhelming. The tears just kept coming as I waited for her to get back. I cannot believe I even asked her to do this for me. The minutes felt like hours as I revisited all the events from the night before.

How could I go from being so disgusted with somebody and wanting nothing to do with them to the polar opposite? And now I was in this boat where it *was* my fault that this happened. It was an indicator of the chaos that was in my brain, how lost I really was, and how I had no self-love at all. I was looking for love in all the wrong places, obviously. I started to realize that my lifestyle would only lead to more of that. I was sitting in my friend's dorm room, and I just had her go to Planned Parenthood for me, and I thought, *What happened to me? How did I get here? Why am I here?* Then, after taking Plan B, I wondered, *Am I committing the greatest sin of all?* While swallowing that pill, I really had to grapple with the fact that I'd chosen this. This happened to me, and this was what I was doing, and now I had to figure out how I would deal with it.

When I went to therapy later in life, I told my therapist that I would go to my grave without telling my mother about what I'd done. I thought, *if I can hide it from my parents, then I don't have to really deal with it.* Again, that was me sweeping things under the rug, trying to bury my guilt and shame. But there are always going to be things in my life that trigger that part of me. No matter how deeply I thought I had buried it or how completely I thought I'd forgotten it, it was there. Later, I ended up having a conversation with my mom about it, and it no longer had power over me. I'm no longer angry about that situation. I have such a perspective about it that I've completely forgiven it, even though I know it's not okay.

I had to live with the consequences of what that was going to do to my life. Even in sharing it now, I know there are going to be people who might judge that situation, but there's so much freedom. I know the saying is that the truth shall set you free. I know a lot of women who have been in the same boat as me, maybe not in the same exact way, but they've woken up, done that walk, debated those same emotions, and experienced heavy guilt or shame over something that they felt was out of their control. Say it out loud, **"I refuse to let shame have any power over me!"**

The truth is that you can be free of all that. Absolutely. You don't need to carry that guilt and shame with you every single day. Even after growing up, getting married, and living a full life, I still have remnants of that same nineteen-year-old girl who carried that. However, I really believe that I'm finally on the other side of the healing process.

There's guilt for doing something wrong, which deserves an apology and remorse, but then there's the guilt you've carried with you for God knows how long. The sooner you identify it and face it, rather than running from it or trying to sweep it under the rug, the sooner you can put it in the box it goes in instead of letting it run around in the back of your mind.

It's important to identify what the origin of your guilt could be. When I first felt guilty for adopting Finley, I didn't relate it to that moment in my life where I experienced the most shame I've ever felt. I didn't realize there could be a connection. So, the next time you feel guilty, ask yourself, *Did I actually do something to warrant this emotion?* Really hone in on it and ask yourself, *Did someone make me feel this way, or did I bring it upon myself?* Dig around with those emotions and allow yourself to go back to your childhood, allow yourself to be in the present, and allow yourself to run through those different scenarios because you need to identify if you're projecting your guilt onto other people or if you are over-apologizing.

*** ACTION STEP ***

If you find yourself constantly apologizing for things, it could be because you are carrying guilt or shame, so much so that you feel the need to apologize for it. It could be that you haven't dealt with some of that guilt or shame. My action step for you is to write down the first thing that comes to mind that you feel guilty or ashamed about.

It could be really obvious to you, or it could be something you have to dig around to find. Is it something that can be resolved in your mind? Can you apologize for this? "The truth shall set you free" is not just a quote; it's a factual statement. Even though new factors will arise from it, it's the only way to progress toward a solution for your guilt and shame. Write a letter to yourself as if you were speaking to a dear friend who made the same mistake or is carrying the same shame. Use words of understanding, forgiveness, and grace. Acknowledge what happened, take responsibility if needed, but speak with empathy, not condemnation.

This practice helps shift your internal dialogue from self-punishment to self-compassion, which is essential for healing. You can't shame yourself into transformation, but you can love yourself into growth, which is an excellent step of hope.

CHAPTER
Eight

BLACK SHEEP, BUT MAKE IT PINK

Online, you might see me as a very positive, outgoing, happy person. Honestly, I had no idea what I was doing when I started growing a following on social media back in 2012—predominantly on Instagram. I try to be someone who always shares the good, the bad, the hard, and the ugly. Kim Kardashian's got nothing on my ugly cry, okay?

I have such a deep connection to the term "black sheep." I identify so much with it, though I don't think anyone would ever look at me and think, *Oh, she's a black sheep*—maybe they would see a pink one (I crack myself up). But there are so many elements from my childhood, as I've shared in previous chapters, about how I felt like I didn't fit in. A lot of people long to be accepted and included, and I think it's one of the reasons that I became such an inclusion advocate for my daughter.

A part of me just wanted acceptance for my inner child. I

wanted to be the girl who made sure everyone felt included because, in some ways, I had been the girl who wasn't.

That said, I definitely participated in some mean-girl activities in junior high. When I made my rounds of apologies, I reached out to a girl I had played a role in making feel bullied. She forgave me and jokingly said I should give her free haircuts as part of the apology—I joyfully agreed. (*And I'm still open to that, girlfriend, if you're reading this!*)

Back in 2012, I started an Instagram account in secret—I didn't even tell Josh. It was my creative outlet, a way to share our story so that when people were around us, they wouldn't pity us. I wanted to keep our friends and family up to speed on our journey with cerebral palsy—the surgeries, procedures, and therapies—while also educating them about everything we were going through. But at the same time, I never wanted anyone to feel even an ounce of pity for how we lived our lives.

The most unexpected thing that happened was that I was able to establish the most incredible connections with other women who were going through the same exact thing as us or were just a little bit behind us in our journey. Just as that mom, Brandi, was there on social media for me when I first started my journey, I got to be that same hope for other people and show them, "Hey, life's gonna look different than you imagined, but it can be even more beautiful than you ever expected." This had so much meaning and purpose for me, and I found that the deeper things that I connected with were actually the ways that I could truly resonate with people. It was never about growing followers, but that's what happened as a result.

I started a social media account called Fifi and Mo, which

documented my daily life with Finley; we did a post every single day. It sort of curbed my appetite for being a workaholic. I found a love for journaling and documenting, and it gave me something else to do than just sit around and be a paranoid worrywart.

I soon found that I'd accidentally built a brand and a niche for myself. I was sharing about adoption, cute mommy and me outfits, and Finley's cerebral palsy journey. However, I wasn't just sharing the hard things; I was sharing how we got through those hard things. To my surprise, it blew up and became this huge window into a whole other life that I had only heard about. We ended up getting lots of collaboration deals and working with major brands like Lexus, Target, Jif, KIND Snacks, DIFF Eyewear, and Funboy.

Our biggest moment was when the Kardashian kids shared a picture of Finley, and it got a lot of negative comments. That was something that really struck a chord with me because, obviously, "Mama Bear" was going to come out. But people had no idea what cerebral palsy was, and I thought it was so cool that the Kardashian kids were featuring her. She had a walker, and it was so refreshing to see someone with a walker being included.

Remember, this was 2015, so it was not something you saw on fashion pages at all. There's so much inclusion and representation out there today, and I feel like we were a part of that little first stone of the ripple effect.

I really believe that the black sheep inside of me was like, *Come hell or high water, I will help the world my daughter grows up in be educated about cerebral palsy.* This is kind of crazy, but my thought was that I wanted to represent cerebral palsy so well on social media that other people kind of wished they had it. That was my mentality. I wanted to make it something that was not pitied or looked down upon. Instead, I wanted people to realize that it's just a life that looks different from theirs.

I also had a blog at the time, which was something that I completely paid for and that I did for myself. I had become a contributor here and there for larger publications. I would blog about different things, and people seemed to be really intrigued by our open-adoption dynamic.

One day, I ended up writing an article about what happened when my daughter was featured with the Kardashian kids. It was like I dipped it in kerosene before I hit "post." It ended up being on the front page of Yahoo and the front page of Google. Huff-Post featured it, too. It kind of went viral around the world and really put our little brand and our little Instagram account on the map. I loved the inclusive side of it so much, and I believe now that that was because of the deep-rooted stuff that I had dealt with in feeling like the black sheep in my family.

Throughout these chapters, I've shared a number of humiliating experiences. I often felt like I didn't quite fit in with my super-smart, type-A family since I was more of a social butterfly.

One of the moments that stands out most about me being the black sheep happened in eighth grade. By then, I had sort of rebounded from all my previous humiliations—just as every kid does. We all have those moments where we have to grin and bear it, and eventually, time moves on, people forget, and you're no longer the talk of the class.

I had started to mature a little, and I had a huge crush on one of the guys in my homeroom class. You'd think I would have learned my lesson about keeping my crushes a secret (remember

Shamu at the pool?) to avoid public humiliation. But I thought, *Surely, this isn't going to happen again.*

I told everybody who I liked, and the news spread amongst the entire eighth-grade class. Word got back to me that he'd told everybody, "Tell Tina..." I went by Tina back then; it was not my mom's favorite thing, but there was another Christina in the class, so I just went by Tina for most of my life. To this day, someone will yell, "Tina," and I'll know it's someone from elementary school or junior high. So, he said, "Tell Tina to ask me out in homeroom on Friday." (I don't remember the exact day, but for the sake of the story, it's Friday.)

I was stoked. "I am so pumped. I am going to wear this cute outfit. This is going to be the day that I get my first boyfriend." That morning in homeroom, I was really nervous. The students sat in alphabetical order, so I was toward the back, and he was right in the front. I got up and marched my happy little butt all the way to the front and said, "Will you go out with me?"

I will never forget the way that he leaned back in his seat so that it was only on the back two legs, you know, like the cool guys did. He turned his head to the side, sort of looked down, and said, "I'm not really looking for a girlfriend right now."

Most of the class erupted in laughter, and a few of my friends' jaws dropped open. I just stood there at the front of the classroom, sort of paralyzed, because this was **not** what I had planned. The door to get out was in the back, and there was nothing funny that I could do at that point.

I darted to the back door, sobbing, and then ran all the way to the locker room. I felt humiliated, and then I had to face everybody for the rest of the day. And it definitely was the talk of the town for a while. That was a very, very hard thing. At that time, there were not a lot of girls asking guys out, so I don't know if I was just ahead of my time, but I definitely felt like a major black sheep because I was one of the first who was really interested in having a boyfriend. I still had a lot of girlfriends at that age who weren't. They couldn't have cared less, and they didn't understand that side of me at all.

In my quest for acceptance, I longed to be included, and I believe that that has so much to do with these experiences of being left out. I know so many people who are good at making sure that everyone is involved and that everybody feels welcome, and they're the most hospitable people I know. Most of the time, when I talk to them, I get deep into their childhood stuff because I can't sit down with anybody and enjoy having a shallow conversation or talking about the weather. I'm like, "Have you been to therapy? Tell me what put you in it." I want to talk about deep, real stuff and have true, genuine connections with others. But when I ask hospitable people, they always say that they felt bullied, teased, and left out a lot—in other words, they were black sheep. I don't think I've ever met somebody who's said, "Oh, yeah, I don't have a problem fitting in anywhere." And if I do, this person is certainly not a mother yet because—just wait.

There are so many different parenting styles and trends, and once you are a mother, you will feel like you are being judged, and everyone thinks you're doing it wrong. I was obsessed with fitting in, and I always told myself, *If I wear these clothes, if I talk like this, if I do [XYZ], then I will feel like I fit in. I will feel like I belong.*

I remember begging my mother to buy me the same brands that my friends were wearing. I longed so badly to fit in and identify with everybody else, even though I was so different, and there were things I really didn't care about.

To this day, I have a thing with fashion that stems from being that super-awkward, hand-me-down-wearing kid whom no one ever wanted to borrow clothes from. Everyone always wanted to borrow everybody else's clothes. So, I love letting my friends borrow my clothes now. That's just something that is very therapeutic for my inner child, and I take a lot of joy in that. I say it's one of my love languages.

There are so many quotes and sayings that basically ask the same question: *Why would you want to fit in when you were born to stand out?* I think, for so many of us, it sounds really cool to say, but when you go to bed at night, when you get back in your car after being out, or when you feel exposed, embarrassed, or like you are a black sheep that nobody understands, it's natural to feel the need to over-explain yourself, to want to get ahead, or just wish that people understood you.

There's so much power in understanding and truly falling in love with yourself, so much so that you don't need anyone to look at you in any other way, and you can almost be proud to be a black sheep. So, why is this important for the reader? Well, one of the biggest things that I preach is that **authenticity is your superpower**. While I used to be ashamed of a lot of the things that make me who I am, I own them majorly now. You will see me singing every freaking show tune that there is and being silly, nerdy, cheesy, corny, or whatever you want to call it.

I love that side of myself, and I have found other people who enjoy it, too. But first, I had to own who I was. There are so many elements of the people we meet, especially as we're in such a heavy social media culture, where comparison creeps in, and we say, *Okay, I need to be more like her.* That's just like our inner child saying, *If I'm wearing that, if I do it like this, if I play on this team, if I play this sport, if I play this instrument, if I take this class, if I have this notebook...* Whatever it is, if you're telling yourself, *If I change myself, then I will be accepted, be happy, be fulfilled...* The truth is just the opposite.

The more you know yourself, the more you will come to love yourself. I'm saying that there are things about you that could be shortcomings, like any kind of struggle that we've talked about in this book, different emotions, or patterns that you have that you wish to change, grow from, and grow out of, but that there are deep-rooted things about you, like maybe you might have a true love of something that other people think is uncool.

What makes you excited? Just because it doesn't make other people so excited, it doesn't mean it's not important. It doesn't mean it's not special. It doesn't mean that you won't find other people just like you. But if you are not sharing and owning who you are, how the heck are you supposed to find, influence, or connect to the other people who are in the same exact situation as you? Don't hide yourself. And don't hide yourself from yourself.

As a hairstylist for almost two decades, I can't tell you how many times I've had someone in my chair who couldn't even look at her own reflection. So, one of my action steps for you is to look in the mirror at yourself. This is something I had to do when I was in the thick of my therapy and dealing with my resentment, different issues, and all the things that made me feel like a black sheep.

The truth is, I didn't know myself, and I didn't love myself. I remember coming across a blog article about a girl who claimed that talking positively to herself and telling herself that she was beautiful in the mirror actually helped heal her skin. It makes sense now, knowing what I do about the way we harbor emotions and internalize things, but what we think and what we say can become our reality.

Remember this rule: If you wouldn't say it about your friend, you're not allowed to say it about yourself. I do not allow people around me to use self-hatred or self-loathing talk. You may think it's not a big deal, but it absolutely is, and every single person who experiences radical growth and change in their life will tell you to knock it off.

*** ACTION STEP ***

Stand in front of the mirror tonight—or even right after you put this book down—and tell yourself that you are beautiful. You can thank God for different blessings instead of being so critical of yourself. Then, instead of pointing out what you don't like, acknowledge what you are grateful for. I certainly struggle with this, but after raising a daughter with cerebral palsy, "Lord, **thank you** for legs that easily get me from A to B." Activate the Reticular Activating System (RAS) of your brain. The RAS is a bundle of nerves at the base of your brainstem that acts like your brain's filter. Its job? To decide what information gets your attention and what gets ignored.

You know how, when you get a new car, suddenly you see that same model everywhere? That's your RAS at work. It's constantly scanning your environment and highlighting what matters to you based on what you've told it is important (consciously or not).

If you're stuck in guilt, shame, or fear, your RAS will filter for more of the same: criticism, failure, rejection. But when you start intentionally focusing on healing, growth, gratitude, and possibility, your RAS begins pulling those opportunities and affirmations into your awareness. You can literally rewire your brain so it will default to hopeful instead of hopeless.

And while you're at it, tell that beautiful soul of yours thank you for reading my book—I'm cheering for you. I have prayed throughout the writing of this entire book specifically for *you*.

Conclusion

As we come to the end of this book, I hope you can look back and see just how much you've grown. Awareness is the first step of growth. Then, you connect the dots from your current life to your childhood for a deeper understanding of why you are the way you are. I know firsthand that this journey has not been easy, and the fact that you've made it here is a testament to your courage and strength. We've talked about navigating:

- Grief of loss
- Heartbreak
- Diagnosis
- Infertility
- Adoption
- Waiting
- Date rape
- Wanting to fit in

- Struggling with gossip
- Numbing and avoiding
- Living with a disability
- Difficult relationships

I hope you feel less alone and more equipped to handle whatever life throws your way now.

Remember, healing is not a destination but a journey, and it's okay if you're still finding your way. Be kind to yourself—progress, no matter how small, is still progress. The challenges you face do not define you; how you face them does.

If you take nothing else from this book, let it be this: **You are capable of rising above your hardships.** You have within you the resilience to face the darkest moments and the light to guide yourself through them. Keep moving forward one step at a time, even if it feels small. Small steps are still steps.

Thank you for allowing me to be part of your journey. This is not the end—it's just the beginning of your next chapter. So, go forward with courage, and remember: You are stronger than you think. These hardships are shaping you for the future, and the journey ahead is full of promise that there is always *Hope in the Hard.*

Thank You For Reading My Book!
DOWNLOAD YOUR FREE GIFTS

Just to say thanks for buying and reading my book,
I would like to give you a few free bonus gifts,
no strings attached!

Scan the QR Code:

I appreciate your interest in my book and value your feedback as it helps me improve future versions of this book. I would SO appreciate it if you could leave your invaluable review on Amazon.com with your feedback. Thank you so much! Xo, Christina

www.ingramcontent.com/pod-product-compliance
Lightning Source LLC
LaVergne TN
LVHW011424080426
835512LV00005B/245